The exact starting point of any major change in society is almost impossible to define, with one notable exception, Elvis Presley's television debut, when he performed "Blue Suede Shoes" and "Heartbreak Hotel" on the "Tommy and Jimmy Dorsey Stage show"

From that moment on, the lives of the American public, including Elvis himself, would never be the same again. America, and later, the western world had undergone the fastest and most far reaching sociological change in history.
Ten years on, and all the old rules regarding morality had been shed like a winter coat, no longer needed in the blazing heat of a brand new summer.

The Naked Hairdresser, "Observations from a shampoo bowl" may shock some, entertain others and possibly enlighten many. Whether or not you agree with the observations is for you to decide, I make no apologies for the explicit nature of this book, I simply and candidly relate the erotic fantasies as told to me by my clients, fantasies, which, on occasion, became reality, sometimes with my participation, if some are skeptical, I can only promise whole heartedly that what I have written is the truth.

I hope these observations will illuminate and generate a dialogue among the populace that will lead to a deeper understanding of the fundamental biological imperative that we all share.

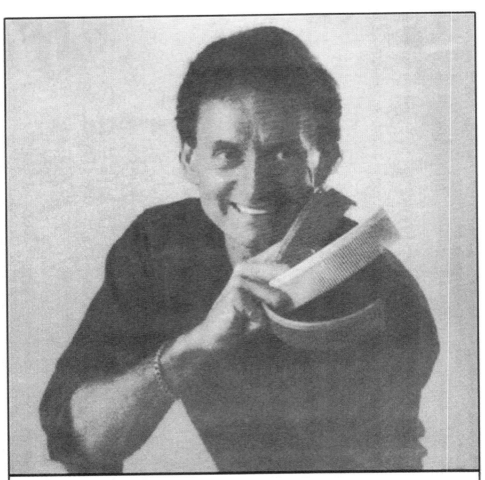

DON DAVIS, CREATOR AND PATENT HOLDER
OF THE GEODESIC FORMAT, CURVE COMB

Don Davis

Paul Mitchell & Jean Paul Dejoria
TO DON DAVIS

I have known Don Davis for about 25 years. Don worked with us in the early days of Paul Mitchell. In those early days, Don was a great asset to us. I consider him an honorable and loyal person.
Good Luck with your book

(John Paul Dejoria Chairman and CEO John Paul Mitchell Systems)

"THE NAKED HAIRDRESSER"

Prologue

This story begins with a birth, mine to be precise, in the small town of Evansville Indiana, on the banks of the Ohio river. The winter of 1936 was the coldest on record, of the previous 40 years, it was a home birth, as was the norm at that time in America, however, as i was in a big hurry to get started with my life's adventure, i arrived a month ahead of schedule, and weighed in at 4 1/2 pounds ! the odds were heavily stacked against me, but thanks to my fraternal grandmother, and her nursing skills, i made it through the critical first three months, being fed with the aid of an eye dropper !

She did such a good job, that i was to stay with her for the next eighteen years.

My generation was obliged to enlist for military service and i opted for the Air Force. Four years later, my duty done, i was in the market for a career, both my father and grandfather were barbers. At that time, there was no barber college in Evansville but there was one that specialized in training beauticians. Fate had decided the route my life was to take.

One year later, my shiny new diploma in my hand, and the certificates of having passed my state examination, i was a fully qualified " COSMOTOLOGIST " ! and ready to set forth on my great adventure.

To my total surprise, the phone never stopped ringing ! ! ALL the leading salons wanted to interview me, after the third one, the bubble burst, and Mrs. Fay congratulated me on becoming the first male hairdresser to graduate in six years.

The beauty salon in " De Jong's " department store was to be my " baptism of fire " into the mysterious world of the female of the species, and it prepared me well for what was to come.

The Salon

A sweet, forty something lady whose name tag proudly displayed the fact that the person it was attached to, could be referred to as " Cathy ", asked if i was lost, i must have looked shell shocked, and i think i probably was , i managed to tell her i was looking for the beauty salon and she instructed me to follow her, we then set off on an unforgettable journey into the unknown through an absolute maze of " Undergarments " I'm sure my face was getting redder and redder with every step, i was Male !, i should not even be here ! finally we arrived at the salon, my guide tells the receptionist that she has found me looking for the salon and asks if she is expecting anyone, the receptionist introduces herself as Alicesteen and asks if my name is Don, i confirm this and she asks me to take a seat. i survey my new world.

Twenty stylists, with ages ranging from thirty to fifty, dressed in white uniforms similar to a nurses outfit, i would be required to wear a doctors " smock ", also in compulsory white, the standard attire for the profession.
While i am filling in the application form i have been given, a very elegant mature lady enters the salon, Alicesteen immediately comes round from behind her desk and greets her with a handshake, i had never seen women shake hands before, and was impressed by the formality. The elegant lady looked at me and engaged Alicesteen in conversation, one of the stylists came into the reception area to inform

the lady that her stylist was ready for her, as she swept past me, i immediately jumped to my feet, she held out her hand and said " I will see you next Thursday " with that she glided past me into the styling room. i turned to Alicesteen and asked " What was all that about ? " she told me i had just met Madam De Jong and i had been officially hired.

The First Day

The next morning, at 09:30, De Jong's doorman opened the door for me and said " Welcome to the family Mr. Don " as i made my way to the salon i wondered " What family ? " Alicesteen greeted me warmly and invited me to meet the staff, she led the way to the back room (all salons have a back room, referred to as the gossip room) Alicesteen introduced me to the ladies who were to teach me the basics of people management, and how to survive with your clients. Without their help, my early years would have been much more difficult.

The first day was tough, ten clients sat in my chair, they were all "society ladies", to use the phrase of the time, this meant they all played golf, tennis, went to parties at the Country Club and participated in various charitable functions. Their ages ranged from late twenties, to fifty something, i found myself engaged in sophisticated dialogue, to say i was un prepared, would be an enormous understatement .

My 2:00 P.M. client told me she was having an affair with her tennis coach, others told me of their new lovers and some reminisced about a previous love, one even asked if i would join her for s drink later, I apologized and told her Monday was my " Work out " day at the gym, what you need to bear in mind here is that i was an un-worldly wise twenty-one year old and had no idea what she was hinting at.

The Second Day

This was the beginning of an insight into the greatest mystery of the universe, the female mind.

10:00 A.M.   Client : Barbara

My first of the day, we would wait outside the changing room to escort clients to the shampoo bowls, she calls to me " Don, i have a problem, can you help me please ? "
" How can i help ?" i ask she replied, " Please come in" the changing rooms had heavy curtains instead of doors, i enter the room.

Barbara is a woman in her early thirties, well toned from hours on the tennis courts, she is 5' 9" 120 Lbs. blonde hair, blue eyes and her zipper is stuck,(one of the great mysteries for us men, is why do they put zippers at the back of women's clothing ? Maybe, it's to make us feel useful.) After a few moments of fumbling with the errant zipper, i manage to release it, as i turn to leave, my mission accomplished, Barbara says, "Don, i would like your opinion." " Sure," i say " On what ? " Last summer when i was in Paris with my girl friends, we all bought French lingerie, i want to surprise my husband tonight as it's his birthday" she stepped out of the dress, i am speechless, she was scantily clad in light blue underwear, with mid thigh stockings, a garter belt, lace "push-up" bra and the first bi-kini panties i had ever seen ! " You look great " i stammered and beat a hasty retreat from the changing room. Giving orders to the shampoo girl to give Barbara a conditioning treatment, i headed for the front desk to tell Alicesteen what had just happened, after hearing my tale, she had some well thought out advice for me, I.E. "Get used to it ! " equipped with this newly acquired, useful advice, i return to the salon to find Barbara is waiting in my chair for me and we discuss her styling requirements, i set to work, after a few minutes, she asks if she could talk to me about something personal. "Sure" i reply, somewhat apprehensively, considering what had happened only moments previously ! With a sigh, she begins her tale, "This is my fifth year of marriage, two wonderful children and a gorgeous husband, sounds perfect, but the problem is, we seldom have sex, maybe twice a month, and i never reach orgasm, before the children, and while we were dating, we just couldn't keep our hands off each other" i could not believe what this lady was telling me, and in such a matter of fact manner ! i regained my composure and said, " Maybe you should talk to your doctor" was all i could think of to say. " I did," she replied, "He just told me sex was not the most important aspect of marriage and that i should try to adjust, fuck that ! i want to feel like a woman, i bought the Kinsey report, have you read it ? " " No" i reply, " You must read it, all my friends are reading and discussing Kinsey's findings"

 NOTE The Kinsey Report was causing scandal in the press and academic circles. As it would later turn out, it was "Kid's stuff" compared to The Masters & Johnson Report.

The following week, Barbara returned for her weekly set and comb out, she was shampooed and sitting in my chair. On the counter i notice a gift wrapped package. " Don," she says, " This is for you, please open it." i quickly remove the wrapping paper expecting to find chocolate turtles, my favorite candy, bit no, i find myself looking at a copy of The Kinsey Report. " i hope you enjoy it" she says.

 NOTE Over the next three years, The Kinsey Report inspired countless conversations with clients.

I finished her comb out and asked if she was happy with it, looking up she says, " I have something i would like to tell you" " Go ahead" i say, I am expecting to hear about a planned shopping trip with her girl friends or something

along those lines. She takes a deep breath and begins
"Don, i go to seedy bars, and pick up men, preferably
traveling salesmen, they have motel rooms, which makes it
easier, my favorite is two men, there is nothing more
stimulating than a Ménage a trios in the afternoon, the
positions lead to great creativity, i control the sex, it's a
great feeling of power, after i have had several orgasms,
for the finale i have them take turns putting their penises
in my vagina and when they are about to cum i take one in
each hand and get them to cum in my mouth at the same
time. I was totally lost for words, this had nothing to do
with a shopping spree ! ! Barbara continued, " This may
sound strange, but there is a difference in the taste of
semen. " i tell her i will take her word for that ! !
NOTE Masters & Johnson stated, in their findings, that women
could recognize the taste of their lovers.

PASSAGES OF INNOVATION

Luck plays a greater part in our lives than all the best laid
plans. When the New York hairdresser Kenneth styled
Jacklyn Kennedy's hair (The Bouffant) she was featured on
the cover of fashion magazines around the world, this
caused a demographic age shift in my profession. Before
the " Boufo" , as it became known, the average age of
clients was late twenties to fifties, over night, this
changed to 60% of the clients being teenagers, salons were
overwhelmed with this sudden invasion, being twenty three,
teenage girls related to me.

Wednesday, 2:30 P.M. Client: Maryann.
She was a writer for the society page in our local
newspaper, observing the sudden influx of teenagers over a
two month period, she had an idea for a story. " Don, i will
talk to my editor about writing on this new trend" (the
Bofu) she called me the next day, the go ahead was given,

to my first 15 minutes of fame, long before Andy
l's famed comment. The article depicted my daily
ɛ, performing my art, and tangible undercurrent in
ılon of the fever pitched sexuality the younger
ɡ- ation was introducing to America. Basically, how it
felt to be a man working in a woman's world.
NOTE: O'Rielly, on Fox News, always criticizes teens
expressing themselves through their fashion, music and dance.
Let us not forget, each generation re writes the rule book,
it has been this way since our founding forefathers made
this possible.

A CLIENT REMEMBERED

She is a senior in high school, her father met her mother
when he was a G.I. stationed in Hawaii, the union produced
what Mitchner, in his book "Hawaii," called "Golden People"
Desire, was and still is, in all my travels, the most exotic
woman i have known, she was 5' 9", unruly flowing black
hair, a willowy form, skin the color of honey and eyes like
Amber, in today's world, she would be a supermodel !
unfortunately, she was forty years out of sync. She coiled
herself into my chair, smiled, and said " I read the article
in the paper, my friends and i drew straws, and i won,
could you give me a "Jackie."
Over the course of the following week, she brought over
twenty friends to the salon which presented a problem for
us, in that they would arrive in groups and shock the
regular clients with their frank discussions regarding their
sex lives.

PASSAGES OF CARNAL KNOWLEDGE

Client : Peggy
Desire had introduced me to Peggy and Joan who were also
seniors at North High. Peggy is in the chair, Desire and
Joan are lending moral support to Peggy to undergo a

drastic change in hairstyle. (which can be a scary experience, especially for a teenager) With everything going well, at roughly halfway through the cut, Desire says "Don, we were wondering if you could give us your opinion on something ?" " Sure" i say, They look at each other, then Joan says ", "You ask him Desire." Overhearing the conversation, the clients on either side of me have gone unusually quiet. Desire plucks up courage to ask " If we have sex with more than one guy between our periods, does that make us whores ? " this is tough, i know not to give a flippant answer at this point, so i say " O.K., it depends on how much you like them and how you feel about yourselves " they seemed pleased with this answer, however, the other stylists and their clients had been eavesdropping and did not approve. When i finished for the day, Alicesteen said she needed to talk to me, and asked me to come to her office, " Don, two clients have complained that you were talking about sex with your clients today." " No " i say, " They were talking to me about it " "Don, please" she said, " We must be careful about other clients overhearing private conversations between yourself and customers. " I apologize and say i will do my best. This was 1960, in the next four years, the fashion world would go from knee length dresses to the micro mini, bras were burnt and the outrageous became normal.

There was a generation gap appearing, the late twenty somethings, and thirty somethings found they were being left out of the newly discovered freedom being thoroughly enjoyed by the new generation, and they were determined not to be left behind.

SODOM AND GOMORAH

Client: Sally.

Sally is twenty eight, 5' 7" 120 Lbs natural strawberry blonde, mother of two, she was my client of one year Thursdays, 3:00 P.M. i am in the middle of cutting her hair, when she asks, "How is your love life ? i'm curious to know, as you work with women all day every day, you must have a lot of opportunities" " Oh no, no" i reply, " I make it a policy never to ask a client for a date" " Really ! how interesting, you live in one of those new apartments on Outer Lincoln don't you ? i have a girl friend who lives there, next time i go to see her, is it O.K. to pop by and say hello ?" " Sure, no problem" i say.

 Eight o'clock that night, my doorbell rings, opening the door reveals a vision in a white silk, mid thigh, off the shoulder dress ! the vision speaks " Hi, i was in the neighborhood so i thought i'd drop by and say hello" she purred as she swept past me into the apartment, " How about a glass of wine, and who did the decorating ? " While getting the wine, i tell her " The furniture is from Salvation Army, i stripped and painted it all myself, the posters were bought from movie theatres " " Show me the bedroom " she demands. Everything is black, with " Lava lamps " for low level lighting. Sally smiles, un zips her dress and lets it fall to the floor, my jaw hit the floor too ! no underwear ! this revelation is immediately followed by the statement :

 " Don, i want you to fuck me out of my mind "
During the next two years, Sally introduces me to ten of her friends, who all became my clients. One at a time or sometimes in pairs, they rang my doorbell, their needs varied, some wanted sex with another woman, some wanted two men at a time, my gym "work out" partner, who was in his last year of college participated when required. He is now a school teacher and shall remain nameless. The

10

common thread through this group, was that they were all
married. This was a first time experience for me with
women of a dominant nature.
In the next four years, both single and married women who
were my clients confided in me and shared their " extra
martial " activities !

THINGS TO REMEMBER

Two major events occur simultaneously at the beginning of
the sixties, one biological, The Pill.
The other, fashion, Mary Quant invents the "Mini skirt"
As with most breakthroughs, it was un intentional, Ms.
Quant owned a dress store in London's Soho, she was having
tax problems and discovered a loophole in the tax laws. If
dresses were below a certain length, they were classified
as "Children's clothing" and as such, were subject to a lower
level of taxation, the rest is history ! Arguably, the third
event was the Bouffant hairstyle, which made salons a
place for all social classes.

The time has come for me to move on, in my last month,
clients have stopped by the salon to wish me good luck for
the future.
Tuesday, two days before leaving, my last three clients of
the day, Debbie, Paulette and Kandy, all three are married
with children, with the exception of Kandy, they have never
talked to me about their sex lives, or questioned me about
mine. The hour and a half was un eventful. Debbie was the
last, she said " Don, we would like to invite you for a glass
of wine." She names a local bar that is well known as a late
evening meeting place for singles, i tell her O.K. i will meet
them in thirty minutes. Checking out at the front desk,
Alicesteen warns me to be careful. " About what ? " i ask,
" I overheard your clients talking they are planning a

surprise for you" " What is that supposed to mean ? "
i ask, " Just be careful " she repeats.
It is only a couple of blocks drive to the bar, so i don't
really have time to ponder Alicesteen's remark.
The three girls are sitting at a booth, the bar is dimly lit
and caters for young professionals who are trying to " Get
lucky " for the night. Approaching them, Debbie slides out
to allow me in, getting me to sit between them, Paulette
and Kandy are on my right and Debbie joins us on my left,
there is a bottle of iced wine in a bucket in the table,
Kandy pours a glass for me and we drink a toast.
The conversation is about my departure and California's
much hyped lifestyle " Don," Kandy says, " Do you believe
communes really exist, where everyone has total sexual
freedom ? " " Yes, they exist." i say, " As to sexual
freedom, you might be surprised by what is practiced here
but not discussed." Kandy re fills the glasses, we drink
another toast, " To life " she says. The girls seen pensive,
finally Debbie takes the initiative, " Don " she begins, " We
have decided to give you a going away party." I ask where,
when, and can i bring someone. They all laugh, and Paulette
says "Oh no, this is a private party, just us and you, in
your apartment will be fine " how could i say no !
On the way out, Kandy picks up two bottles of Champagne,
Dom Perignon, (What else !)
The next morning on the sun deck of my apartment roof,
four naked, tired and extremely happy people watch the
sun rise. To paraphrase Hemmingway, it was a movable
feast.

SIX MONTHS BEFORE THE FAREWELL PARTY
Client: Kandy
She is twenty eight, 5' 7," slender, brown eyes, short
brown hair and the mother of a five year old girl.

Occupation : Co - Owner of an antique furniture store with a girl friend.
Wednesday, 3:30 P.M. appointment.
Kandy is debating highlights, " What do you think, will it make me look younger ? " " Yes," i reply, it will soften the color of your hair " " Let's do it " she decides.

This is a two hour process, and my clients usually use this as an opportunity to talk about their lives. Twenty minutes later, Kandy has still not said a word, i ask her why she is so quiet. " Don, May i ask you something personal ? "
" Of course" i reply, " Before i was married, there had only been two lovers in my life, one in high school, and the other in college, since i have been married, there has been no one else, and i feel as if life is passing me by. " " Stop feeling sorry for yourself" i say, " You could easily pass for twenty " " Thanks " she says, " I needed that, Don, i'm going to be blunt, i have this fantasy, it's about you " she hesitates, this is the kind of pause in a conversation where you become aware a bridge has been crossed in terms of relationship between people, she lets her breath out and continues, " Don, i should like to make love with two men at the same time." " This does not shock me " i tell her, " Other clients have shared this fantasy with me. " she says, " I want you and your friend *Bob, he is your " " Work-out " partner am i right ? " " Yes he is , but how did you know about that ? " she says " A friend, who shall remain nameless, told me about an incredible erotic experience she had with you both " i smile and tell her " This may or may not have happened " " Could we make it happen next Friday night at your apartment ? "
" Are you sure about this ? " i ask, she says yes, " O.K., done" i say.

Kandy's hair is now finished, she pays her bill, walks back to me, and puts her hand in my pocket to leave a tip, and whispers "Get some rest, you're going to need it. "

Kandy arrives Friday at 7:30 P.M. she is wearing a little black silk Chanel dress, 4" Stiletto shoes that are guaranteed to drive men crazy, her fragrance, Estee Lauder. Frozen Margaritas have been poured and sipped. Herb Alpert and the Tijuana brass are on the stereo, the lighting is subdued, one red spotlight enhances her pale white skin. Kandy speaks, " This is my party, and you will do as i say " *Bob and i readily agree. " Sit on the couch and watch " Kandy moves to the center if the room, she sways to the rhythm of the music, reaches behind her and unzips her dress, it falls over one shoulder, revealing a black lace bra, the other shoulder is dipped, and the silk dress slithers down her body, i envy the dress on it's journey down her body, caressing her leg and falling to the floor. Daintily, she steps out of it and hooking the dress with the toe of her stiletto, deftly flips it onto the air and onto my face, i find i am transfixed, the smell is intoxicating, the primitive aroma of a woman in heat ! Kandy calls out in a guttural, commanding voice for us to remove our clothes and join her in the dance, Bob and I do as we are told and surround her, naked bodies swaying together in a ritual like movement of primitive lust and desire. At her command, we remove her bra and bi kini bottoms , *Bob has dropped to his knees and slides them off, she steps out of them and places one very long leg over his shoulder and guides his mouth to her vagina, " Lick me " she begs " I want your tongue deep inside me." Bending forwards, she tells me go down on my knees, then, reaching behind her, she spreads the cheeks of her arse and orders me to lick her.

Time has lost all meaning, we are no longer three separate beings, we are one entity, she tells us to stand and she drops to her knees between us, the slender fingers of her left hand with their red lacquered nails encompass *Bob's penis and her right hand holds mine, she places first one at a time, then both together into her voracious mouth, sensing we are close to the point of no return, she rises and leads us to the bedroom, which is illuminated by U.V. lighting (popular in discos at the time) resulting in her skin glowing iridescently.

Lying on my back, Kandy has mounted me, she leans forward and guides *Bob into her rectum, she tells us to ejaculate into her at the same time, we do our best.

We relax and listen to Kandy describe her sensual pleasure and enjoyment of the night, we rest, then continue with every possible variation three people can think of, some with great difficulty.

FINAL COMMENTS

We had no swinger clubs in Evansville, open marriages were unknown. The women who shared their bodies and fantasies with me, did so not in a mechanical, emotionless way, we respected each other deeply and cared for one another. This was to change, and has the become the limbo which young people find themselves in today, i will attempt to relate how that came about in the following chapters.

THINGS TO REMEMBER

In the sixties, sexual preference was openly discussed in the salon between clients who were not acquainted and often of different social backgrounds. To my knowledge, there has not been a definitive study on the contributions the beauty salon industry had on the exploration of alternative lifestyles. Perhaps this work will inspire such a study.

CALIFORNIA DREAMING

My bags are packed, the "427 Corvette" is roaring, looking back in the rearview mirror, the city of my birth fades into the distance. Like doors in time, as one closes, another opens ahead of me. I was part of a great exodus, in the mid sixties, the youth of America left the small hamlets and headed for the bright lights of the big cities, they were like one homogenous mass, seeking, with the fervor of religious zealots, the new "Mecca" the "City of angels" with it's Spanish origins would never be like other American cities.

The great distance between east and west coasts, in a more primitive time, assured autonomous development. Los Angeles and "Angelinos" are criticized for lacking character and identity, the pundits of negativity declare " No one is real there," this writer would prefer to say they are more mike the Chameleon, in that they constantly re invent themselves as needed.

HOLLYWOOD, SUNSET BOULEVARD

From " Whisky a go-go " in the west, to " Green Blatt's deli " in the east, 24 hours a day, an estimated 100,000 young people maintain a constant motion in the same unfathomable consensus, they traverse in a clockwise movement.

The "Aware Inn," the setting sun has cast glowing rays on the hills of Hollywood . Sitting at an outside table, sipping a glass of wine i think of the beat generation. Paris in the nineteen twenties, would have found kindred spirits in Jim

Morrison of " The Doors " Sonny and Cher, Ike and Tina Turner, Janis Joplin, the poets, the tunesmiths and writers all participated in the great mandello that was " The strip " the greats rubbed shoulders with the not so greats, shared roach clips and acid trips. For me, fashions, hairstyles and make up were inspiring.

The gods are with me, two exotic creatures are watching me from the next table, they are dressed in the native costume of Romanian gypsies, long black hair, festooned with flowers, leaving, they stop at my table, the glorious Californian sun is behind them and the transparency of their clothing leaves no doubt that they are totally naked beneath it. One nymph speaks. " Hi, my name is Moonbeam, and my friend is Stardust, we were wondering if you have a crash pad ? " "Yes " i answer, " Why do you ask ? " "Perhaps you would like to join us for a spiritual awakening "

Five minutes later, squeezed into my car, i follow directions that lead through winding roads. In Laurel Canyon, Stardust tells me to turn into the next driveway, at the end , a 1920s mansion that had once belonged to a star of the silent movie era, stood in decaying splendor awaiting our arrival. These places were mostly rented to self proclaimed " Gurus " and holy men representing esoteric cults. Bella Lugosi would have approved, more a castle than a mansion,

complete with turrets, and vents for pouring molten pitch on parents seeking wayward daughters. The "Vette" is parked, as we approach the door, there is a brass gong on a stand, Moonbeam picks up the beater and strikes the gong, the resultant sound reverberates throughout the castle, luckily, molten pitch does not rain down on us ! thus, we are accepted, slowly the door opens in true " haunted house " fashion. We are greeted by what must have been the double of " Rasputin the mad monk " he welcomes us, Stardust performs the introductions, the " Mad Monk " turns out to be the Guru, my Astro Guides lead me to a huge room, thirty feet high beamed ceilings, seventy five feet long, by forty five feet wide, fireplaces at each end burning logs, candles dimly illuminate this cavernous interior, the flagstone floor is softened with Persian carpets. Long tables, painted black and supported by bricks two feet high, and randomly scattered Bean Bags complete the furnishings.

FEAST OF THE SENSES

A gong is sounded and the inhabitants appear in groups of two's and three's, and take up positions on the scattered Bean Bags. The surreal atmosphere is added to by the fact that everyone is silent. A chime rings out and the Guru appears, wearing a black and red floor length robe, he glides to the center of the room , lifts his arms and begins to chant " NO MNE OHO ORINGE KE " the assembly joins in, after three minutes, a chime is struck, and once again silence reigns. Two naked girls enter the room they circle the Alcoats, who's head is bowed, three times, whilst continually striking the chimes. The Guru then takes his seat on a large Bean Bag and the two naked girls arrange themselves either side of their master. A distant chime sounds from what i later discover is the kitchen, a line of men and women arrive carrying bowls of fruit and bread, they circle the room three times then place the bowls on the long tables, soft Indian music is reverberating around the room, coming from concealed speakers. The feast ended with " Joye's Delight " there was a palpable air of anticipation for the event that followed.
The Guru bids everyone enjoy the night and departs with an arm around each of his girls. This signaled the start of the mating ritual, the females make their choice of partners.

From an untouched bowl of various fruits, they select, and insert the item into their vagina, and returning to the men, straddle their faces, and hidden by their robes , the fruit is eaten, sighs of pleasure fill the room, Stardust and Moonbeam have decided the three of us will join in with the ritual, " Rites of Venus ", offerings of strawberries and grapes are " served " and consumed. Never was a feast served from such delightful vessels !

I visited the castle for three weeks, partners were mandatorily changed each night, the women always made the choice, some became clients.

COMMENTARY

The commune was a transitory phenomenon, by the seventies, they had lost most of their popularity. On the surface, confrontation was geopolitical, the Vietnam protest, Racial equality, Recreational drugs. Women's empowerment was mainly ignored.

This dynamic was soon to be challenged, inequality of pay and the " Glass ceiling " were twenty years in the future. Beginning in the sixties, female sexual equality bore fruit by the end of the decade.

BEVERLY HILLS SALON

The salon was a franchise of the Glemby Co. located in Imagnum, the staff, including myself, numbered ten, four men and six women, i was the youngest, the clientele was " Old Hollywood ", to me, this meant anyone over thirty. The receptionist recommended me to the younger clients, they should try the " New guy ." Oddly enough, older hairdressers were rejecting Vidal Sassoon's revolutionary new techniques, the younger clients were soon requesting me. Through word of mouth, i was becoming fully booked, this is hard to understand, even Beverly Hills salons, as well as the rest of the beauty industry were un aware that a major change had taken place. Set, teased and under the drier, had gone the way of the horse and cart era.

On my first day, i cut and blow dried 12 clients, every one of them a " Shag " request. As i was leaving, Molly, the receptionist, informed me they were getting requests for the new guy who could cut the " Shag " and do something called a blow dry.

NOTE : This was before "Sassoon" opened the Rodeo Drive salon.

A generation of young people was lost to the salon, not because they didn't want hair care and styling, but because they did not want their mother's " Army Helmet " style. This will never happen again in our profession, on-going education provided by the Paul Mitchell company, will prevent this. In future chapters, the concept that keeps our industry vibrant will be addressed.

My clientele expanded explosively. Before blow drying, the average number of customers per day was around 12, following the introduction of the new technique, that figure at least doubled.

HAIRDRESSERS MAKE THE "A" LIST

Fashion magazines emphasized that if you did not have a hairdresser at your party, it was not on the "A " list. Clients began contending for my presence at their parties. A typical Beverly Hills / Bellaire / Holmby Hills party had the hottest new bands performing, poets reciting modern day poetry, artists painting psychedelic landscapes on nude models. Drugs like Pot, Uppers, Downers, Red devils and Yellow Jackets were plentiful, Coke came later.

Sex was mandatory, both private and public, the combinations rivaled ancient engravings found on temple walls in Asian cultures, put simply, everyone did everything to everyone else !

BEVERLY HILLS LADIES WHO "DO LUNCH"
The "Luaul" Hawaiian restaurant on Rodeo Drive.

On entering, you are transported to a Mitchner-esque landscape, native girls in sarongs, flowered " Lays " draped around their necks, guide you across bridges over streams fed by waterfalls. A primordial mist gently caresses an abundance of tropical flora. The Luaul may look like a Hollywood set, but it is more famous for it's menu, exotic drinks, and as a rendezvous for lovers, bored wives, (whose husbands are the movers and shakers of the film world) to parade their paramours, to be seen but not seen, between the hours of twelve and two, the ladies who " Do lunch " then, in a feeding frenzy, depart in Mercedes, Rolls Royce, and Ferraris, to hide away love nests.

 In conversations with other Hollywood hairdressers, prolific numbers shared this information with their stylists.

SWAP CLUBS
There were numerous " mate " swapping clubs in Hollywood, places where one went alone, anticipating a new adventure for the night. My favorite, " The Citadel " was an inter-racial club owned by a famous actor.

LADIES OF POWER
Client: Ms. Garret
She is a rising, thirty something studio production executive, a very stylish, trim woman of exceptional intelligence. She is having her hair blown and styled.

" Don. " she says, "Maybe you can help me, as you know, i work twelve hours a day, which leaves little time for a social life, i must attend a cast party at " The Daisy " (a venue on Rodeo Drive famous for it's cast parties) would you consider escorting me ? " this is a no-brainer ! i tell her it would be my pleasure. " Great," she says, " Let me have your address, and i'll pick you up at eight."

I am wished well by all twenty of my clients of that day, having told them of my invitation.

In tinsel town, emphasis is placed on the last film you made, or the last party you attended.

There were no set rules for fashion in the sixties, my outfit for the event was white silk shirt with ruffled front and cuffs, black velvet vest, black velvet bell bottom pants, with black suede boots. Indian silver Concho belt, silver necklace and bracelet, both inlaid with turquoise and coral, all authentic Navaho.

8:00 P.M. Ms. Garret has arrived in a black stretch limo, the chauffer looks like " Odd Job " from the film " Goldfinger "

NOTE : Hugh Heffner hosted a Playboy T.V. show, the girls who were regulars on there started a fashion trend, that became Designer wear for intimate events. The girls wore Vanity Fair sleepwear as clothes (Victoria's Secret is great, but why keep it a secret ? flaunt it !)

Ms Garret was caressed in a Vanity Fair white, clingy, shorty p.j. that was at least eight inches above the knee, the bodice was a white lace translucent cloud, spaghetti straps struggled to keep her encased ! A simple white pearl necklace, a thin white gold Rolex on her wrist, ruby red nails and lip gloss, a dusting of silver glitter on her hair and shoulders and four inch white satin covered heels. Ms Garret was a vision !

" Don " she says, " At the party, feel free to do whatever you want, i must schmooze the investors " " No problem, don't give it another thought " i tell her.

" The Daisy " awaits, paparazzi are swarming, flash bulbs going off like fireworks. " Odd Job " opens the door, Ms. Garret takes his hand and two extremely long, bare legs extend out from the limo. Hollywood reporters flock, microphones are thrust, questions asked and answered. One even asks me who i am ! i reply " I'm her hairdresser " and my picture is taken.

The cast party consists of actors, actresses, directors, producers, all the people involved with the production of Hollywood " Magic " the pilot was accepted and enjoyed a five year run. This was my first cast party, but by no means my last !

The night had just begun, parties are great business opportunities for people in the fashion and beauty industries, fashion is an ice breaker, never offensive, and always controversial, a good way to gain new clients, i would, every now and than, catch a glimpse of Ms. Garret usually deep in conversation with one or more of the " Money people ". Twelve thirty, she taps me on the shoulder and informs me that it's time to leave. The limo is waiting at the curb, we board and depart before the paparazzi have a chance to catch her.

The limo is equipped with a bar, Ms. Garret pours a glass of Champagne, hands it to me and pours one for herself, we chink our glasses, " Don, the night has just begun, as you know, i don't have time for romantic pursuits, however, my sexual needs must have an outlet, there is a club in north Hollywood, will you accompany me ? " " Yes, i'd be happy to " i tell her, she smiles, we touch glasses again " Thank you " she says " You won't be disappointed "

To my surprise, we have stopped in front of a famous

" swap club " owned by a famous 50s character actor, it is a renovated warehouse, the bar, purchased from one of his movies, circa 1880 New York Bowery set. Ms. Garret seemed to be looking for someone, she spies a secluded booth occupied by two well known couples. " Wait " she tells me, " I'll be right back " five minutes later, we are in the limo heading for Bellaire. To enter Bellaire, you had to be invited, evidently this was not a problem, as the guard waved us straight through.

Our destination, deep within the enclave, we come to a stop in front of a pseudo 17th century Chateaux, we approach the massive oak doors and they swing open as if by magic, (i learnt later that they were electronically operated). We enter a room that looked as if it could host a soccer match ! Thirty foot high beamed ceiling with brass chandeliers giving a subdued illumination. Scattered throughout the room were islands of " over stuffed ", leather furniture. At least fifty guests, many of which, frequently adorned the pages of movie magazines and gossip rags. A whisper in my ear told me that when i wanted to leave, the limo was at my disposal. Wandering through the room, i am invited to join various groups, they ranged from couples, to the largest group, which was a party of six. As the saying goes, " When in Rome " the emperor Caligula would have been envious ! My five mile run the next morning was an ordeal !

Ms. Garret ? . . . . . the last time i saw her, she was in a large bed with four other people of various sexual orientation.

IN REMEMBERANCE

The best kept " non-secrets " were the assignations that took place in the " Lual " restaurant. It became famous when Lana Turner's daughter killed her mothers boyfriend who was abusing her mother, he was the Maitre De for the restaurant . Rumor has it that Richard Gere's breakthrough movie " Beverly Hills Gigolo " was based on the activities that took place in the " Lual ".

I   MEET   A   DOMINATRIX

Client : Cliest

Cliest is a producers wife, she is thirty five, 5' 6" one hundred and fifteen, well sculptured pounds, we are discussing changing her style, " Don," she says, " I want something different " her hair is light brown, shoulder length. " I just discovered that my husband has brought a Mercedes convertible for his new mistress, i want to shock him, what do you suggest ? " " This will be fun " i say, " How about we cut it real short, and tint it black, this will enhance your blue eyes ? " " Sounds wicked." She replies, " Let's do it " One and a half hours later, a metamorphosis has taken place, her hair is jet black, slicked back close to her head, glancing in the mirror, she says, " I love it, this is a new me. If you have no plans for tomorrow night, i promise a surprise ! " " No plans " i say, "Good, i will pick you up after work " The next day was very busy and i totally forgot about Cliest, at seven fifteen, the receptionist calls me to the front desk, she hands me a folded note that reads . . . pick you up out front at seven thirty. This gives me just enough time to clear my station, brush my teeth and head for the front door. There is a yellow Bentley convertible parked at the curb. " Hop in " says Cliest, (Never say no to ladies driving convertible Bentleys !) Pulling away from the curb, we take Wilshire West. Cliest smiles, " How do you like my ensemble for the night ? " she asks, " In a word, hot ! " i say, she is *dressed in tight black leather pants, black leather vest with silver buttons down the front, no bra or blouse to distract from her magnificent breasts, mid calf black leather boots with 4" heels round of the outfit. " Where are we going ? " i ask " Sit back and relax, it's not far " she says, We leave Beverly Hills, traffic is light, five minutes later, we are winding through Mulholland Drive. I am thinking, this road is famous, Errol Flynn once had a house here. Turning off, we traverse a lane between magnificent trees that line the road, high overhead; their branches intertwine in the breeze like lovers arms caressing each other. The house appears as we leave the lane, designed to mimic an early Spanish mission. As we leave the car, Cliest squeezes my hand and says, " Please keep an open mind " We stand in front of two Rodin-esque bronze doors, figures in base relief suggest " Dante's Inferno " a huge iron striker rests on an iron plate, Cliest tells me to lift it and let it fall, doing so, the resulting sound thunders through the mansion, momentarily the doors slowly open, and standing before us is what i can only describe as a woman of Amazonian proportions . At least two inches taller than me, what i can ascertain of her form, mostly hidden by a Caftan, is formidable ! she bows her head and bids us follow her. The hallway is both long and wide, the light fittings on the walls have electric bulbs designed to imitate flickering flames, strangely, this is my most vivid memory of the night ! Midway down the hall, we stop in front of double oaken doors, reinforced with iron bands, our guide pushes open the doors, and gestures inside, the dimensions are difficult to make out as the lighting is once again the flickering bulbs of the hallway, and barely illuminates the room and people assembled therein. A large, circular, black sheeted bed is surrounded by ten, occupied, black leather chairs, the people on them are attired in black Caftans, making it impossible to establish their gender, i am* thinking, the " City of Angles " must be the prime market for Caftan sales ! Gregorian chants begin to fill the room, i could not tell where they were coming from, as the speakers were concealed.

The Amazon walks to the bed and removes the Caftan, it is the emergence of " Venus on the half shell ", her pale white body shimmering with dynamic power, completely shaved from head to mound of Venus, a well oiled apparition in flickering light. Cliest moves towards the bed, and in a commanding voice, orders the Amazon to lay on the bed, she meekly complies with the instruction, from one of the seated " Caftans ", Cliest is handed four black silk scarves, Cliest holds up her arms and asks " Who will assist ? " four " Caftans " rise, and approach the bed, each are given a scarf, two go to the head of the bed, and two to the foot, Cliest commands them to bind her. The Amazon is spread eagled on her back as the scarves are knotted at her wrists and ankles. Secured to anchor bolts on the floor, she is immobile, the " Caftans " return to their chairs, yet another one holds out a black whip with braided flails of silk. Cliest circles the bed caressing the ivory body gently with the whip, she stops, and without hesitation raises the whip above her head and powerfully strikes the quivering body, this is repeated five times, as she circles the bed. The Amazon is moaning, not with pain, but with ecstasy, the whip returned, Cliest walks to another seated " Caftan " the object handed over is an incredible black rubber dildo. (John Holmes must have been the model !) returning to the Amazon, she runs her hands over the long white thighs, reaching the apex, her well oiled fingers gently probe the vagina and anus, Cliest slowly caresses the inner thighs with the phallus. The Amazon pleads, " DO IT, DO IT ! " the dildo is placed in the waiting vagina and with slight pressure is slowly engulfed by the voracious opening. Cliest begins a pumping motion and the assembled

" Caftans " chant in unison " Faster, faster " the Amazon is screaming for more.

Not wishing to become repetitive, every orifice receives the same treatment, over the next two hours, using every conceivable sexual device and the participation of the " Caftans ".

We did not speak on the return drive, Cliest was in a high state of euphoria, she dropped me off, at my car and drove away. I knew on her next appointment, all would be explained.

Three weeks later : 4:30 P.M.

Client: Cliest

She is in my chair, the explanation begins;

"Don, thank you for not questioning me, the group of which i am a member worships the Egyptian Isis, what you saw was, we believe, the ritual of fertility as performed in the ancient temples of Isis. We perform this once a month; the other members are wives of professional Hollywood movers and shakers. Some are your clients but i can't tell you who, no one ever told me they were there.

Cliest left me a big tip, i was never invited again.

Information you might find interesting, the ancient Egyptians removed all body hair using wax, modern women use wax and now laser, with which there is no re growth.

COMMENTARY

California was one of the first states to make it legal for sex therapists to have " Therapeutic " sex with their patients, without fear of prosecution.

Playboy magazine published information about people who were charged with sodomy when these acts took place in their own homes. A case in Texas, where police broke into the wrong address. They had misunderstood their informant, however, the two male tenants were caught engaged in mutual sexual gratification, they were arrested and charged with sodomy. This case brought others to light. Playboy magazine paved the way for the " Consenting adult " act when practiced in private. Hugh Heffner is owed much for his courageous stand.

THE ELYSIAN FIELDS

In the late sixties, the canyon adjacent to Los Angeles, became a fertile ground for exotic retreats (the E.S.T. institute) **Transcendental Meditation** (Mahrishi) **Flower Power** (The Elysian Fields)

Timothy Leary, the Harvard professor who introduced L.S.D. to his students, claimed a transcendental experience took you to higher dimensions. In an interview before his death, he admitted he just wanted to have sex with young girls.

 NOTE ; The present Fox News channel reports daily about the abuse of young girls by older men in polygamist cults.

Clients are telling me about new retreats where you can attain higher planes of awareness. America had embraced a whirlpool of hedonistic exploration, this would change with the "Yuppie" generation, more on that in future chapters.

Client : Marge

Single Beverly Hills real estate agent, Marge is my 4:00 P.M. appointment, she is shampooed, conditioned, and waiting in my chair. " Hi Don, how's your day been ? " " Fun, as always " i say, " How about you ? " " Great " she says " Lets do something soft with my hair, i have an important viewing later, they are from Iran, and i want to be Conservative " " Good idea " i say " Make sure your skirt is below your knee, maybe you should wear black, they will think you are in a Chador." she laughs and says

 " Maybe that's a good idea, my Olga Cassini will work " i do a soft, face framing cut and suggest understated make up. An hour later, Marge says " Wish me luck " and with that, leaves.

Understated make-up. An hour later, Marge says "Wish me luck" and with that, leaves.

It has been a long day, my last client just left and the receptionist calls me from the front desk, " You have a call " she says, and hands me the phone. " Hello, to whom am i speaking ? " i ask, " Don, it's Marge, your hairstyle did it, i sold the house ! Don, do you remember our conversation about Elysian Fields ? " " Yes " i reply " Why ? " " i never told you but i am a member, would you like to be my guest Sunday ? " "Sounds good " i say " Where will we meet ? " " Why don't you pick me up 10 : 00 Sunday " " O.K. " i say " Give me your address " Luckily, Marge lived in Beverly Hills, not far from me.

Sunday, up early, two mile run on Santa Monica beach, back to the apartment, shower, shampoo, quick blow dry to the hair. This is my " Indian " period, shoulder length hair, Navajo print shirt, brown leather vest trimmed with beadwork and fringe around the edges, bell bottom jeans and Indian moccasins.

NOTE : - 25 years later, my mother informed me that my great great grandmother was a Cherokee, i was fully entitled to wear Indian clothes !

10 : 00 Marge's condo, the doorman rings her apartment and tells me she will be down shortly. Two minutes later the elevator doors open, never having seen her dressed informally, i almost did not recognize her ! she is wearing a long flowing multi colored silk, sari off at one shoulder, a string of prayer bells in a long loop around her neck chime as she walks towards me, bare feet, ankle bracelets with chains linked to toe rings a long black wig, heavy " black out " lined eyes and the ubiquitous red dot on the forehead, she would not have looked out of place on the streets of Calcutta " Do you think i look like a temple Al-coyote ? " she asks, " Never having seen one " i say " You should be acceptable " Marge laughs and says " Why don't you follow me, then you can leave when you want " i am waiting in my car as she emerges from the underground car park, she is driving a bright red Porsche 911, forty-five, hair raising minutes later (she should have been the first woman grand prix driver !) We arrive at Topanga Canyon, still sparsely developed (unlike today) many "Western" movies used the place as a location. After leaving the main road, we wind through a landscape strewn with boulders created by the last ice age! Ten minutes later, deep within the canyon, we have arrived .the architecture can only be described as " Tinsel Town Gothic " twenty or thirty very expensive cars are parked under a canopy of giant eucalyptus trees, Marge parks and i pull in next to a

Lamborghini Muir, Marge is waiting for me at a drawbridge that spans a fifteen foot dry moat, sensing my apprehension, she takes my hand and says " Don't worry i'll protect you " we both laugh, having crossed the drawbridge, we approach the gothic façade, to my surprise, when Marge pushes the doorbell, the soft sound of harp music surrounds us. The door silently opens and any anxiety i felt melts away, in front of us stand two Sari robed girls with garlands of flowers woven into raven tresses, the girls hug us and spray incense of roses over us to " purify our beings " apparently, they circle us three times chiming small bells, purification complete, we enter the temple, Marge places one of the girls hands in mine and tells me she will be my guide, she leaves us and my guide says " My name is Tamara and i will instruct you in the three Light Paths of Pleasure " holding my hand, Tamara leads me through sparsely furnished rooms, with an abundance of potted ferns and plants of every color of the rainbow. A heavily draped door confronts us, Tamara parts the drapes and we enter. It is a changing room, ten people of different sexes are shedding the last vestiges of the outside world and donning saffron robes, under which, the bodies are naked, some i recognize as T.V. personalities, the muted conversations are light and convey no clues as to status in the world we have temporarily abandoned. Tamara's assistance made my transition from the mundane, external world to this Garden of earthly delights a pleasant one, she approves of my transformation and once again takes my hand and leads me through roofless passages flooded with golden sunlight, soft Indian music completes this ambience of well being.

THE SANCTUM SANTORIUM

Having entered the heart of the retreat, the outside world is no longer relevant, i feel clothed in sensuality, this euphoric state, on my part, has not been reached with the aid of "enhancing substances". Other people are now entering the room, ten in all, table mats comprise a large circle, and our guides seat us in the Lotus position, incense burns in brass pots around the edges of the room. A gong is sounded an un earthly silence descends on the room, from an unseen entrance, The Master enters, he walks, through a diaphanous cloud of incense, to the center of the circle, he claps his hands and ten temple guides enter, they circle The Master chanting "OM OM OM "he raises his arms and once again silence reigns, with the deep resonance of his voice reverberating through the room, he speaks. " Welcome to the temple of love, let your hearts embrace fulfillment, leave all earthly inhibitions aside, this will be a day of spiritual *awakening, place your body and spirit in trust with your celestial guide, enjoy the fruit of your being " A gong is sounded, The Master departs,*

NOTE: The Guru was dressed in a hooded caftan so i can't describe his features, a year later his picture was in the L.A. Times, he was arrested for dealing in L.S.D. he had been employed as a used car salesman in north Hollywood. In L.A. nothing is as it seems!

The music has changed now, to "Ravell's Bolero" guides position themselves next to the Insiate_they are assigned to instruct, Tamara stands before me and removes her robe, she is slender, and there are no tan lines, underarm legs and pubic area are all completely shaven. This was very unusual, the sixties was a time when hippie females did not shave at all, legs or underarm let alone pubes! This "hygienic" rebellion was embraced by mainstream society, they thought, this was being natural.

The other guides have now removed their robes, and they too are shaven. Tamara assists me in removing my robe, and gently massages my neck and shoulders she leans forward, lips to my ears, and in a husky voice, whispers to me to lie on my back. Glancing around the circle, we seem to be synchronized as if choreographed with a silent command, Tamara tells me to close my eyes and empty my mind of thoughts she says to picture a garden, you are lying under a Lotus tree, as the wind blows, Lotus blossom gently descend and kiss your body. I could feel the blossoms as they kissed me from head to feet then paused and began again, velvet caresses on my lips, i taste the nectar of flowers, she moved with a deliberate symmetry of motion, i feel hot breath between my thighs, a wet tongue licks it's way up a very aroused shaft of carnal hunger, i am engulfed, i have been drawn into a bottomless maelstrom, before i can release the elixir of life, contact is abruptly broken, fearing abandonment, i open my eyes, Tamara lifts her head, smiles and says " Everything is as it should be, this is the first step towards Karma i will now tie a silk scarf over your eyes, you must feel with your inner spirit ", she wraps the scarf around my head, beginning to relax, time has lost all meaning, without a focal point, substance is abstract. fingers massage my body, gentle yet with yearning, two warm pillars of flesh straddle my head, i smell the fragrance of fresh oranges, a mucus mouth of life caresses my lips, timidly, my tongue explores this offering, the sweetness of forbidden the fruit Eve gave to Adam. The rhythm becomes faster, my tongue plunges deeper into this well of eternity. A new sensation! i feel a weight slowly descending on my

43

44

hardness, fingers grip my shaft and guide me through layers of flesh, a rocking motion of power, reaching a frenzy, keeping pace with the final crescendo of the "Bolero" my mouth is filled with a sweetness more than honey, essence of life has burst from my shaft and fills the crucible of life. Slowly, my senses return, moans of pleasure fill the room, time has stood still, a tongue begins caressing my tumescent_penious.

The hours of paradise have not abandoned me, fire is building in my blood, like the Phoenix from the ashes, i have risen, my hips are straddled, and once again guiding fingers do their work and direct me into a hungry maw of flesh. There is a difference, the tunnel is a smoothness of wet heat, and it is not ringed with the ridges of grasping flesh there is no rhythmic pelvic motion, squeezing of vaginal

muscles, moving in a masturbatory motion. NOTE: this technique was practiced in Hindu temples carved stone phalluses were used, supposedly, to aide in birth. The pressure builds, and i explode in a euphoric state of surrender, could this be what the poets of the Kama Sutra called the "Small Death".

Once more the wheel of time has come full circle, Tamara ever so gently removes the silk scarf blindfold," Don? "She asks, "Was the astral plain journey fulfilling? "" It was Nirvana "i tell her, she smiles happily, offers her hand to assist me to my feet. Never before or seldom since have i felt such utter depletion of self, looking round i see my fellow "travelers" being assisted with loving care by their Astro guides. Oddly, i am beginning to think of them with this frame of reference. Tamara takes me on an exploration of the retreat, she tells me each room is a path toward final awareness, my room was the first step on the path, "How long will it take to reach the final path?" i ask "I don't know "she replies "Each path is different for each traveler, only The Master can tell you when you are ready for the next path "I could see that this might take some time and be

expensive!. Wondering where Marge might be, i ask Tamara if she could help me locate her, She says " Let's check the refreshment lounge " without Tamara, to find anything would be impossible, through a labyrinth of hallways, people in different modes of dress and undress gravitate toward mutual destinations. We enter an open gallery, bubbling fountains and vases of flowers fill the space with perhaps twenty people in groups of mixed sexes, some in muted conversation, others on bean bags amorously entwined. I spy Marge, she is reclining between two exotic creatures robed in white diaphanous gowns, they seem to be sharing an intimate interlude,

Marge spots me and waves me over, " Did you find initiation interesting ? " she asks, " Very interesting " i reply.

"Marge" i say, "It's getting late, tomorrow is a busy day for me at the salon, i should go, are you staying? " "Yes "she says, "Before you go, i want you to meet my companions, they are Light and Amber. " It was easy to tell which was which, Light is a Scandinavian blonde with light blue eyes while Amber was a brown skinned beauty of Egyptian decent, cat like deep brown eyes, flashing with mystery. "Don" Marge says, "This was my first experience of the temple of Lesbo", whereupon she turns to light and gives her a deep kiss then Amber and repeats the caress, Amber says "Sure you wont change your mind and join us? " "It is enticing, perhaps in the future" i reply, Goodbyes said, Tamara leads me back to the front door and kisses me goodbye.

On the drive back to Hollywood, the events of the day run through my mind, all in all, a most enjoyable experience. Two similar events occurred within three months, i was the guest of two clients, both un connected, client Joan, took me to a temple in Coldwater canyon, Client Sinthe, to one in Laurie Canyon. There was little difference in the activities, leading me to think perhaps there is a handbook on " How to operate a Love Temple " these were the only three times i visited and participated in the rituals at Love Temples.

IMPRESSION

The enclave of Beverly Hills is a " Golden Cage " the inhabitants are enclosed in a mystical womb nourished by the aspirations of ten millions people wanting to get in.

FOOT NOTES

Most of the so called " Gurus " were out of work door to door salesmen, some had success, E.S.T. became very popular, some led their followers to disaster (Charlie Manson)

SIXTIES END

Manson and his so called " Family " has sounded the death knell for the decades final gasp. Their senseless rampage of murder sent a chill through Beverly Hills, police stop the long haired and unwashed, at the city limits and send them back to whence they came. Clients are coming to the salon with body guards. With tension running high, and daily smog alerts, the magic of Hollywood is fading.

SIXTIES IN RETROSPECT

The sixties was, arguably, the most turbulent decade in American history since the great depression, our inner cities, long neglected, burned with racial strife, disappointment with government and the Vietnam war, filled the streets of America with the youth of our country. Martin Luther King led a million people on a march to Washington and gave a speech equal to Lincoln's Gettysburg address. We lost some of our best, John and Robert Kennedy, Martin Luther King and the heroes who died in Vietnam. But we also had great accomplishments " One small step for man, one giant leap for mankind " is now one of the most famous phrases in modern history, marking the first moon landing. Through all that happened, the good, the bad and the indifferent, Elvis had returned ! the status quo was maintained.

THE BOOKS THAT SHAPED OUR LIVES
"Catch 22"   "Valley of the dolls"   "In cold blood"   "On the road"

THE MUSIC
"The Beatles"   "Bob Dylan"   " The Doors"   "The Carpenters"

THE MOVIES
"Easy Rider"   "Lolita"   "Candy"

There was no nudity, no full frontal, we progressed to using " forbidden " words on screen.

ON STAGE
"Hair"   "Oh Calcutta"
These two set the standards, and lowered them !

REFLECTIONS
(The fashion impact)

There should be studies done and degrees awarded in " Fashion Sociology ". What we wear and the hairstyles we favor say more about our emotional state and political beliefs, than volumes of books by authors in " Ivory Towers "

50

HAIR   (my field)

The bouffant of the late fifties / early sixties, broke with the
traditional role of women's " Conservative housewife ", coiffeur.
The mid sixties " shag " reflected the new sexual freedom of women,
they had the right to explore. By the end of the sixties, the look
had become androgynous, driving down Sunset Boulevard, it was often
impossible to tell, from a glance, who was male and who was female.

HAPPY PASSAGES
The Renaissance Woman

Once again, the 'Vette, the power of it's roar undiminished, is conveying me to a new realm of opportunity. Like H. G. Wells' time machine the 'vette seems able to cross frames of special dimensions, perhaps it is endowed with an innate ability to perceive change, the ruptured chaos of dead dreams lay behind, San Diego, in all it's innocent beauty beckoned.

Rita has invited me to her enchanted cottage on Sail Bay. I arrive early on a Sunday morning, "Hobbie Cats", with sails unfurled; gently glide on aqua blue, undulating waves. The enclave boasts one cottage, three houses and an apartment complex. The inhabitants, who are of both sexes and diverse professions, these 'Beachnicks', i am later to discover, share their pot and on occasions, their love. The roar of the '427 brought everyone out of their habitats.

Rita, "model" thin and tall, is jumping around like a Mexican jumping bean in a green bikini. Having parked in front of her cottage, we hug for the next five minutes, when emotions finally subside, she informs me that the cottage is all mine, she has moved into one of the apartments with a girl friend, Rita tells me to unpack later as we are having breakfast at " World Famous". The restaurant is about four blocks away and while walking there, we meet a friend of hers, who

decides to join us, his name is George. George is the beach, clown and practical joker, we became friends. "World Famous" is on the Board Walk, the customers are dressed casually, lots of bikinis, tie-dye shirts, sandals and well worn jeans. Over breakfast, George questions me about my plans, i tell him that "Jerry Magnium", an up-market clothing store in fashion valley, needs a manager for their Salon, which is a franchise of the "Glemby" chain, and i have an interview Monday. As we walk back to the cove, i am impressed by the apparently healthy lifestyle of the locals, people are walking, running, riding bicycles, NOTE : this was before rollerblades and skateboards. *a few were roller-skating. Activity has picked up, "cook out" fires under Habitchi pots filled with roasting meats, vegetables and fruit add their aroma to the salty, on shore, breeze . Rita helps unload the "Vette and tells me to put on a swimsuit and look for her on the beach. My first day is wonderful, i go for a ride on a catamaran, and meet people very different from the L.A. beach community, these people are far more "laid back" and seem to be less "driven" to have a good time. Over the next month, i learn beach romances are "of the moment", if they become more serious, they*

move in together usually off the beach and return just for parties
NOTE : had Margaret Mead studied the San Diego "Beach nicks" mating habits she would have found it un necessary to travel to the South Pacific.

First week in January 1970, i meet the Glenby Co. regional representative, Ms. Broom, at the salon located in the "Jerry Magnium" fashion center, Fashion Valley. After a short interview, i was hired as a working manager, this meant that the company did not have to pay you to manage, my duties, sweep the floor, fold towels, fill shampoo bottles, supervise the other stylists, promote the salon and also, cut hair. I LOVED IT ! !
The salon was locked in the stone age ! the stylists were still doing shampoo and sets.
Including me, the salon had a staff of three. This was going to be a challenge, the smallest number i had worked with before was fifteen
My first day, we assemble for a staff meeting, all three of us !
Patty is twenty three and June is twenty four, i state that from now on there will be no more shampoo and sets, we will train with models until we are proficient in the Vidal Sassoon method of precision cutting and blow drying. Patty asks me about their regular customers, "We will convert them", " Don," June says, " We are both single mothers and scared. " i have checked the books, both of you average ten clients a day, in three months, you will double that. " i was wrong, it took ONE month.

RENAISSANCE

For the next three days, the salon will be closed, we will work on models only, " But Don" Patty says, " How will we get these models ?" " We will use the Jerry Magnium staff ". " They will be our walking advertisement."
The employee lunch room is full, approximately thirty people, both men and women. i ask for their attention, introduce myself and explain what i need, and ask for volunteers, there are none, i obviously have my work cut out, (no pun intended) " Fashion wise," as i explain, "San Diego, like the rest of the world, is going through a search of "Self," the entire fashion world has lost a generation, Mary Quant, from her small shop in Soho, has been the only new fashion statement in the last decade. The "Flower children" and Hippies mainly invented their costume from things they put together themselves, some from Salvation Army and goodwill stores. What is selling to the young, is found in small boutiques."

Everyone has stopped eating and i now have their un-divided attention. Again i ask for models, the store manager stands up " You have one." she says, with that, the room begins to buzz, the men's department manager asks " Is this just for women ? " " No " i say, we are unisex, everyone laughs. A girl who works in the lingerie department asks " Can i bring my boyfriend, he is a pre-med student ? " his hair is long and he knows it needs styling but does not want to go to his dad's barber." " Bring him in. " i tell her " No charge" he can be a model. NOTE, he is now the leading plastic surgeon in San Diego. That afternoon, eight Jerry Magnium employees request a style change.

The Jerry Magnium store manager, is a striking woman of forty something, her hair is teased and heavy lacquered she is a bit nervous " Don " she says, " Do you mean i will have to shampoo my hair every day and blow dry it ? " " Yes, think about it, you take a shower every day, your hair should be just as clean as your body " " O.K. but if i have trouble blow drying, will you help ? " " Sure, come in before the store opens, and i'll teach you."

 The procedure was repeated with all the volunteers for one week, after that they learnt the skills to perform their own blow dries. Three days later, Ms. Brady, the store manager, joins me for lunch. " Don " she says, last night at my literary club meeting, my friends could not believe you could run your fingers through your hair, without disturbing the style, i demonstrated with simple brush strokes, and the hair returned to it's original style. They will be in to see you." " And if i may," she continued, " You have made a new friend, in my husband. " " How so ? " i ask, " We never make love on the day i have my hair done, this new method has changed that." NOTE: for the next five years this was heard from clients of all ages. This small freedom has been entirely overlooked, as one of the important factors that simplified women's fashion and led to autonomy in the bedroom, and the boardroom.

The phone is ringing off the hook! fifteen to twenty clients a day has become normal, the problem is, i have to teach the stylist how to cut and blow dry. NOTE: No schools in America were teaching Vidal Sassoon's new method, unfortunately, it would take the beauty industry another ten years to catch up.

There was also another, not so quiet, revolution taking place in the adult entertainment industry. Prior to this, " Adult " movies were referred to as "skin flicks" and not screened in mainstream cinemas. The Broadway successes of "Hair" and "Oh Calcutta" were changing laws and attitudes, entrepreneurs sued the courts for the right to take the "Adult" movie out of "men only" clubs <u>V.F.W.</u> and go mainstream. It had always seemed strange to me, that men, seem to underestimate women's curiosity, firmly believing, that women would be offended, and not want to see this sort of thing.

Client : Susie, is a trim, thirty year old mother of one, her husband, also a client, was to become a good friend. Susie is having a cut, her hair is naturally curly, we have decided on a long layered style, letting it dry naturally. Don" she says, " You wont believe what my friends an i did last week, as you know, i am the chair woman of the San Diego doctors wives organization (The most prestigious hospital in San Diego which will go un named.) " This is what we did, we rented a bus which had a bar on board " " What was your destination ? " i ask, " O.K. here it comes, we went to L.A. to see "Deep Throat" (" Deep Throat " is the talk of the salon) with Linda Lovelace, it was so exciting, the oldest of our group was fifty five, and all she could talk about on the way back was the surprise she was planning for her husband ! " he was head of neural surgery at another hospital, which shall also remain nameless.

"Don" she says, " When my husband has his next cut, ask him if he thinks i have improved." "Susie" i say, "You could probably teach Linda Lovelace a thing or two ! " " she laughs and says " My girl friends and i have found it difficult to get past the gag reflex." and she proceeds to tell me how Linda Lovelace performs Felacio on men with really big cocks, completely engulfing them " She goes all the way down until her lips touch his testicles. have you seen the movie ? " "No " i say, but my girlfriend saw it in New York" Susie asks, " Did she demonstrate the technique for you ? " i laugh and say, " No, but she is doing her best " we both laugh.

COMMENT

The reason myself, and other San Diegans had not seen this movie, was because the city government made it illegal for theatres to play XXXX rated movies in our fair city. "Playboy" fought in courts across America defending the " The first amendment " that people had the right to make up their own minds about what they deemed "Art" and not be told by a government agency, what they could and could not see, or read. I had clients of all ages who did not approve of this movie, but the overwhelming majority thought that viewing should be a personal decision.

NOTE : Elvis, during the height of his popularity, was refused permission to perform by the mayor of San Diego ! America's fairest city has much changed.

Client : Doc. Jeff 1 : 30 P.M.
Jeff is getting his hair cut and is happy. " Don " he says " Susie told you about her expedition to see Deep Throat,

59

well it was money well spent ! she has been practicing every night and in a few more days, i think she will have it. i have told my golfing buddies about the movie, and three of them want Susie to organize another trip for their wives. (she did)
The salon is swamped ! we are getting upwards of a hundred calls a day ! and to add to the problem, one of my two stylists informs me that her husband is being transferred and she will be leaving at the end of the month, i am desperate.
It is Monday, nine o'clock, we open at ten, i have come in early to do the books. The store manager calls me and says there is a girl who says she is a stylist and wants to apply for a job, she pauses, and says " Don, i don't think she has the right image for "Jerry Magnium" "so," i ask "what is wrong with her ? " she says " The girl is a flower child," "send her up, i will take a look." Two minutes later there appears before me, the personification of a flower child. Long straight red hair, a white, off the shoulder, puffed sleeve, cotton blouse, faded, ripped, bell bottom denim jeans, Jesus sandals, Love beads and the ubiquitous "Peace" sign on a leather thong tied round her slender neck, in fact, being 5' 6" 105 pounds, she was slender

60

everywhere ! What else can i say, we got on like we had known each other for years. Her name was Lori.

A DISAGREEMENT

The Glemby company informs me they will not pay for an assistant training program. NOTE : A year later, the Glemby company are to launch a training program featuring John and Suzzie Chadwick, our paths are set to cross in the future with the Paul Mitchell company. *Lori and i discuss the problem, she tells me there is a new salon in a new building, half a mile from Jerry Magnium. The next morning, i check it out, the salon was on the second floor of a well designed and landscaped building. If you have ever visited San Diego, you were probably pleasantly surprised at the harmonious blending of nature and commerce. Walking up a wide, sweeping stairway, i pause to absorb the vista, mountains frame fashion valley, the old Spanish* mansion built by the catholic monks, lies a mile to the south, to the east and north, freeways span the valley, designed to mimic Roman aqueducts, indeed this freeway system has achieved international acclaim. Two well dressed ladies are walking towards me, "Excuse me" i say, "Do you happen to know where the salon is located ? " " Yes" says the one in the light brown "De' Larentia" dress " We are going there, come with us" the "De' Larentia" asks, " Are you a hairdresser ? " " Is it that obvious ? " " You look the arty type " she says, " Where did you come from ? " " Beverly Hills, but as of recently, Jerry Magnium, fashion valley." Reaching the salon, i open the door for them and follow them inside. The décor is pristine French, light blue, with white and gold highlights, the name " Beau Monde" translates to "Beautiful World" .

The regal looking lady behind the reception asks the ladies who their friend is, The De' Larentia smiles and says " We found him wandering around looking for the salon," " Introduce us " the regal looking lady says, " This is Barbara and Jean, my name is Mrs. Toner, and you are ? " I'm Don, i'm a hairdresser, and i would like to have an interview." " Why don't you have a seat." says Mrs. Toner, she turns to Barbara and Jean and asks how she can help them, " It's an emergency, our club has a meeting in two hours, could we have a wash and set ? " Mrs. Toner looks nervous, " Let me check the book, i'm sorry, your regular stylist has clients and everyone else is fully booked, it will be twenty minutes before a stylist is available." she tells them, approaching the desk, i say " Excuse me, perhaps i can be of assistance, if they agree, i would be honored to do their hair." before Mrs. Toner can ask them Jean says " That will work." Barbara nods her head, " Yes " Mrs. Toner says " We have a vacant station and you can use the equipment to set their hair " " That won't be necessary." I say, " A brush and hand drier will be enough."

" While they are being shampooed, follow me to the station to see if you have what you need." She says. The station is typical of that time, lots of rollers for setting. " There is a problem, no blow dryer." i say, Mrs. Toner says nothing for a moment, then asks " Why do you want a blow drier ? " " Mrs. Toner, You have an English accent, surely you are familiar with Vidal Sassoon's new method ? " " I have read about it." she says, " Our manicurist uses a blow drier for drying nail polish, ill be right back." Barbara is shampooed and sitting in my chair. " Don" she says with a mischievous smile," Do what ever you want with me." Mrs. Toner is back with the blow drier, " Can you do both of them in an hour ? " " Yes " i say

" But why take so long ? half an hour tops ! " The equipment is not the best, but it will suffice, ten minutes into the blow out, the salon has come to a standstill, clients and stylists are watching in rapt fascination. From start to finish, fifteen minutes and Barbara is finished. " Would you mind modeling while i blow out Jean ? " She walks through the salon, clients want to touch her hair, " No hairspray ? " No teasing ? " some ask her to shake her head, and are surprised to see the style fall back into place. Fifteen minutes later, and Jean is finished, they change from smocks back to their dresses, on the way out, they stop by the front desk to pay. Mrs. Toner says " No charge, and thanks for being models." She, is a smart business woman i think to myself. Barbara walks over to me and slips her hand in my pocket, they thank me again, and depart. " Let's go to my office and talk." Says Mrs. Toner. She has a nice office, antique desk, stuffed leather chairs, with the same motif as the salon. Mrs. Toner asks " What did she put in your pocket ? " putting my hand in i pull out a note, folded over two twenty dollar bills, reading the note, i tell Mrs. Toner " You might find this interesting." i say, handing her the note. She reads it and looks up, the note simply said; Our friends at the club meeting will want their hair blow dried. " What will you need," she asks, "Today is Monday," i say " Next Monday, i can start" she agrees, we shake hands, as to my needs, four stations and two assistants" "Why two assistants ? " she asks " I have an associate, her name is Lori, she is also proficient in the Vidal Sassoon method." she thinks for a moment, " We have an area in the back of the salon it has a view of the freeway and the south side of Fashion Valley " " We will make it work." i tell her. " Now tell me about yourself." she begins, " I have been in the beauty business fifteen years, worked my way up to manager in a salon in Mission Valley, NOTE : The salon was a rival chain to Glenby Co. My assistant manager and i decided to go into business for ourselves, ten stylists came with us and five from another salon joined us, we also have six manicurists. " What is your work schedule ? " she asks, " Tuesday through Saturday 10 A.M. to 8 P.M. with assistants, one client every fifteen minutes, that's an average of thirty five or forty a day. Any questions ? " Mrs. Toner has a dubious look on her face, " Do you really think you can do this ? " she says " Yes i can, for three months, at Jerry Magnium, with one assistant, the average was twenty five a day." " How do we find the assistants ? " she asks, " Why don't you call the beauty schools, tell them we are interviewing, and to send us their recent graduates."

She says " One other challenge, we need a meeting with the staff, they will be uneasy with this arrangement." " O.K." i say, " Will it be possible to call a meeting tomorrow after work, Lori and i will address any queries they might have, and explain our plans for implementing the Vidal Sassoon method, perhaps some will be interested in learning the technique." " I will go to work on this," she says " and have a business plan tomorrow night this is a major change in the industry, i have been reading about Sassoon, but to be honest i had my doubts, but after having seen your work this is exciting." We shake hands, and i leave.

THE MEETING

Lori and i have discussed in depth how we can initiate the training program that will benefit "Beau Monde's" staff, we thought they would embrace the new format with enthusiasm. We were in for a shock !

07:30, P.M. we arrive at the salon, Mrs. Toner greets us warmly, and asks us to join her in her office, she says " We have a problem, only 5 stylists said they were interested, if you would rather not give a demonstration, i would understand." " No " i say, " if only one will stay, then that's the one i am interested in " Three male stylists, Robert, the youngest, is twenty four, Bob, thirty and Paul, thirty six. Two female stylists, Veronica thirty one, and Sonia, twenty two. Oddly enough, all the manicurists stayed. Mrs. Toner introduces us, " If one of you would volunteer for a cut and blow dry, the technique will be self explanatory." No one does, without hesitation, Mrs. Toner volunteers herself. While she is being shampooed, i ask if anyone is familiar with the geometric format. Paul responds, " Yes, i have been reading in the trade magazines about Vidal Sassoon's methodology, if i understand correctly, the clients will come in every five or six weeks, how can we survive ? " " Paul, think about it, with the old system, 50 to 60 clients a week is normal, but the problem is, it's the same ones every week, with the new format, six hundred in six weeks is attainable." Bob asks how we can get that many clients. " There are millions of people in San Diego county, at this moment, Lori and i are the only hairdressers who use this method. " that got their attention !

Mrs. Toner is ready. " Everyone please come closer, and don't hesitate to ask questions." They gathered round the chair and remained silent throughout the procedure.

Looking in the mirror and admiring her new style, Mrs. Toner asks " What if i can't do this in the morning." " Don't worry, Lori and i will do it for you until you learn to do it for yourself." Veronica says, " None of us have blow driers." " Let me suggest that tomorrow, you call all the beauty supply houses, surely one must stock them, remember, this method is a blueprint, comparable to building a house, you will be able to duplicate any style once you have mastered the method." " Veronica asks Lori " How long did it take you to learn ? " " About a month in all, i worked every day on models, they were store employees, so they became walking advertisements for us, why don't you do each other so the clients can see the change." " Are there any more questions ? " i ask, there are none. " Keep this in mind, Lori and i will give you all the help you need. Thank you for coming to this meeting, we will see you next Tuesday." Mrs. Toner invites us to her office, she asks us to take a seat and if we would care for tea, we both accept the offer, she goes to a small table in the corner of the office, on which, sits a silver tea service, she fusses over the preparation, ritual accomplished, she takes her seat behind the desk. " The tea will take a few minutes to ' Steep' " she says. " I must be truthful." she begins, " The reason the other stylists did not attend the meeting was because they were protesting against you two joining the staff here." " My partner thinks you will cause distention in the salon," she holds up her hand to stop any comment being made. " However, last year i visited my family in London and made a point of going to Vidal Sassoon's salon for a pedicure and manicure, i was fascinated by the quality and quantity of their work, i have another question for you, did you tell your existing clients you would be here from next Tuesday ? " " I told a few that i had seen the salon and thought it would be a good location for Lori and myself, why do you ask ? " She smiles and adds " Are you ready for your tea ? " we nod agreement and are served tea in fine bone china cups complete with a basket of scones, Mrs. Toner returns to her seat. " To answer your question " she says, " We have had at least fifty calls asking for appointments with the two of you." Lori and i look at each other with great relief. She also says, " 'Something Mad' is telling their customers to call ' Beau Monde' this surprises me, " Mrs. Toner, i didn't know this, one week ago when i prepared their models for a charity show, you may have seen the write - up in the San Diego Times. "Don, please forgive me" she says, " I didn't make the connection." " No problem." i said, " I told them i was re-locating and they must have told their clients." " How's the tea? " she asks, we both voice our approval. " How shall i book the people who are calling ? " Mrs. Toner asks, " Let's do this, for the first week, just give them the days we will be here and the hours we will be working, and invite them to come in at their convenience ".

" But don't you want a definite appointment schedule? " Mrs. Toner asks. " Yes, but not the first week, this will help you to understand the rhythm and flow of this system." . Tea and scones devoured, Mrs. Toner walks us to the door, i am surprised to see Robert, Sonia and Veronica sitting in the waiting area, Sonia stands and says " We want to thank you again and we are looking forward to working with you both." " A personal question " says Robert, " How long have you been using this method ? " " A little over two years, i was lucky, a hairdresser from England shared an apartment with me in Hollywood, that was how i learned " Veronica asks, " How old are you? " Thirty four " i say, " Why? " " " We thought you were in your early twenties, you are the same age as us" " Does that help ? " i ask, she smiles and says " Yes " Lori and i bid everyone farewell. In the parking lot, Lori says " I think this will be fun." i agree, we both have dinner dates, so we say goodnight.

COMMENTARY

For those of you who are reading this tome purely for the salacious content, the preceding chapter no doubt disappointed you. This is a lesson not to be ignored, The beauty industry was in crisis, we had lost a generation of youth, the human spirit strives best when confronted with adversaries. In today's world, Americans find themselves challenged with out sourcing and an energy crisis. Ours is the most adaptable culture on the globe, this adaptability we owe to our prime resource, the emancipated American woman, in cultures where women are denied equality, all suffer equally.

My Tennis shoes are tightly laced, i have donned my Gold's Gym sweat suit, my leather lifting belt is cinched around my waist, the clock reads 06:00 on a cloudless San Diego morning. Leaving my cottage, i walk the twenty feet to the beach, pause for a moment, inhale deeply and commence my run. Five miles will be covered before i finish.

I have rounded Sail bay, and approach " Hamills " famous surf shop. The landmark wooden rollercoaster of Belmont park recedes to my left as onward i run, approaching the Mission Bay causeway, the boundary, to South Mission Beach, surfers in black neoprene wet suits, appear as sea creatures, sitting on surfboards paddling out in search of the elusive, " perfect " wave, some, their boards tucked under their arm, are walking towards the sea and give me a " Hi - Five," the salute is returned. Reaching the furthest point of my run, the turn is made and my route retraced. The nexus of mind and body commences, endorphins pump, there is a no pain, plateau of thought reached, beyond comprehension in a sedatory state.

NOTE : all who routinely exercise, are familiar with this feeling of euphoria.

Belmont park, it's wooden rollercoaster taking on the shape of the fossilized remains of a long extinct creature, is left behind, crossing the street and making my final turn, my companions are a police cruiser and a garbage truck P.B.'ites not yet awake.

The last half mile is a full out sprint. Walking along the beach as i cool down, one adventurous Hobie cat has put to sea, it's sharp keel breaks the surface as an on-shore wind fills it's sail. Just another normal morning for those who inhabit the beaches of southern California.

THE MADNESS

The first day at Beau Monde, it was predictable, Lori and I were swamped with clients, by the end of the week, we had established a productive system, and more importantly, fun.

The next six months sped past without any memorable client based conversations, one day, in the back room, on a break, Lori says " You know, we have been so busy, I have not had time to get to know my clients." As usual, Lori was able to define a problem before I became aware of it, " Yes," I say," Something has been missing, and I think you have put your finger on what it is." Simple solution, we slowed down and began to interact with clients like before.

THE BARBIZON ADVENTURE

Barbizon modeling agency, opens a branch in San Diego.

An earlier client, Penny, former fashion model, becomes a teacher and executive consultant for Barbizon.

Client : Penny 3:00 pm. Thursday.

This is Penny's tri-monthly sun-streaking appointment.

" Don " she says, " I have a proposition for you." " Always open to a proposition from a beautiful lady." She smiles and says " Later, this is business." " What ? " i ask, she says Barbizon needs a consultant

for hairdressing, several members of staff have recommended you.
" Tell your boss, i'm definitely interested " " I knew you would say
that, is Monday for lunch at Barbizon O.K. for you ? " "Tell them i
will be there. " i say, she looks in the mirror. " After the meeting,
if you don't have any plans, i'm working on a project, we could discuss
it over a glass of wine " " Sounds interesting " i say. During the
next half hour, Penny tells me about her second husband (she will
marry twice more !) " Don " She says, " John told me last week,
he wants a divorce." " He must be crazy, you are incredible ! " i
exclaim. At 5' 9" green eyes, beach volleyball fit, she was. "John
tells me he is gay, if he was bisexual, we could work on it but he told
me that after much soul searching he could no longer have any
feelings for a woman. "Gosh Penny ! i don't know what to say" i
stutter." No, it's O.K. you know he is a very successful surgeon, and
is prepared to give me the house in La Jolla and a big settlement,
the only thing he asks is that I don't tell." She hugs me, and says "
See you Monday."
Monday noon, Barbizon, fashion valley. Arriving at the reception desk
and introducing myself, Helen, the receptionist, says "Mr. Volger and
the staff are in the lunch room, please follow me." My first
impression, understated décor, very elegant and large. The lunch
room, eight people seated around the room in conversation. An
elegantly dressed 40 something gentleman approaches me, extends his
hand, we shake, "Call me Ben" he says, thanks me for coming, takes
me by the arm and introduces me to the staff. My affiliation with
Barbizon proved to be an exciting three years, some clients became
more than just clients !

An excellent lunch, catered by " The Butcher Shop", a premier San
Diego eatery in fashion valley. Barbizon's coordinator of events, asks
me when would I be available to do a seminar. "Monday is my day off
" i inform her " I will call you to confirm, a week Monday " she says
" That will be fine " i reply. " Tell everyone i enjoyed the lunch and
am looking forward to our association." Penny is waiting by the front
door, " Why don't you follow me" she says. I'm thinking, no problem
for a 427 'Vette. We are off, Fashion Valley road to 405 north, 80
miles an hour, her blonde hair streaming in the wind, La Jolla drive to
Moorland, several sharp curves later, we turn into a well shaded lane,
the house sits back 50 yards from the road, it is early Spanish
California. She jumps out of her car and says " I hope I didn't drive
too fast." " I managed to keep up " I say, her car was a Mercedes
450 SL. She takes my hand, we enter the house, The foyer ceiling

was twenty feet high, a spiral stone stairway led to the second floor. " Come with me " she says, still holding my hand, we ascend the stairway to a white carpeted hallway, massive doors of bleached Wormwood stand open, a very large bed with white satin sheets, and red satin pillows beckons, Penny turns, puts her arms around me and kisses me softly. " Why don't you pour the wine ? " she says, indicating a silver ice bucket on a low table next to the bed. " I will be right back " Two glasses of excellent Rhine wine are poured and waiting in long stemmed crystal. Penny has returned in a white, off the shoulder, silk gown, slashed to both hips, two very long, exquisitely formed legs flash with a tantalizing preview of what is to come. She extends long delicate fingers with Carmen red nails, gently she accepts she glass. Angeline Jolie red lips, part seductively, she sips the wine gently lowers the glass, placing it on the table without breaking eye contact, she cups my face in both hands, leans her body against mine and whispers, " Don't be gentle" the bedroom has a ceiling covered in mirrors.   NOTE : in the future when i build my house, i borrow the idea.

2:00 p.m. Wednesday:

Client : Ruby.

She is a rare specimen, a native born Californian and by decree, she is tall, thin blue eyed, one problem, her hair is light brown. On her last appointment, I suggested highlights, this more natural new method has an interesting origin, an unknown surfer was hanging out on the beach and somehow came into contact with a lemon, not being able to eat it, he, being a genius, squeezed it in a Newtonian epiphany, on top of his head, the acid in the juice, combined with the endless Californian sun did the rest, instant highlights. The fad quickly spread beyond the surfing community, clients begin asking their stylists for "Sun Streaks" the challenge was met, and a technique improvised, the result, natural California blondes, even if you lived in Keokuk Iowa !

Client: Ruby.

Ruby is a third year business major of University College San Diego. " Don " she says, " My sorority sisters are waiting to see how this turns out " " Let's not disappoint them" i say. While Ruby is processing, she tells me her friends want to do something with their hair," Maybe you could do a presentation at the sorority house " Will they give me permission to do this ? " i ask, " Yes, we have guest speakers once a month. "

The moment of truth has arrived, Ruby has been shampooed and conditioned, she wants to keep her hair long, I have cut it in long layers, sounds simple today, but layers in haircutting gave stylists a format in which to create exciting new shapes. Blow drier in one hand, and with the other, I fluff Ruby's hair as it dries, it begins to curl slightly the finished result resembles a loins mane.

This is what is so good about the world of fashion, nothing has to make sense, a Lioness does not have a mane, only the male Lion, however, this style became known internationally as a Lioness mane.

Clients and stylists have surrounded my station I tell Ruby " Please shake your head" strands of gold shimmer in the light as if struck by a sunbeam , to my amazement, everyone applauds. " Don" Ruby says, "I will call you and give you a date for the presentation" she kisses me on the cheek and says "My sorority sisters will love my hair, see you soon" The next day, I am called to the front desk, i have a phone call, this is unusual, we never use the business phone for personal calls. It's Ruby, "Hi Don, everyone has gone crazy, they all want my hairstyle. Are you available for Thursday night?" " Yes, I will bring Lori" " Is there anything special you will need" she asks, "Just volunteers, and can you give directions to the receptionist" saying goodbye, I hand the phone to the receptionist and return to my client. Her name is Pat and she is fashion coordinator for an up market department store in fashion valley. " Sorry for the interruption" I say, and explain what it was about. " Have you ever done this before?" she asks, " No " I say "Not for a sorority, but I have done presentations and assisted at fashion shows, why do you ask? " she says "Let me know how this turns out, it gives me an idea" My association with Pat will become very interesting in the future.

University College, San Diego, Thursday, 7:00 p.m.

Lori and I have finally found the sorority house, Lori presses the door bell no more than a minute passes before the door is opened, a forty something trim woman greets us with a warm smile and says " You must be our guest speakers, please come in" we find ourselves in a large tastefully decorated foyer our greeter extends her hand, and shakes first Lori's then mine. " My name is Mrs. Higgs, the girls are waiting in the rec. room, before Ruby introduces you, the girls will sing their sorority song. Please stop by my office when you finish." Ruby joins us, " Hi Don, Lori, thanks for coming, are you ready? " " Let's do it." The rec. room was down a long hallway as we approached the double French doors, i could see it was filled with bean bags, overstuffed couches and to my shock, sorority sisters in every state of dress and un dress ! Sweat shirts with

Bikinis, shorty P.J's Terry cloth robes and men's shirts, all barely covering the bikini bottoms. Ruby is laughing, " Come on Don " she says as she opens the doors, " They won't bite you, besides, you have seen girls casually dressed before" " Yes, but not so many at one time." Lori is laughing now, " Come on, time to go to work " she says. i sheepishly follow them into the room.

Ruby asks the girls for their attention, the buzz slowly subsides, " Don and Lori are our guest speakers for this evening, they are from Beau Monde and will be advising us on the importance of hair grooming.

Let me digress for a moment, these young women filled the room with scholarly gravitas, radiating an intoxicating freshness. This was a glimpse of what the future held, they would be the Yuppies of the next decade.

The lecture was short, basically on how important a part fashion played on job interviews, simply stated, you only have one chance to make a first impression.

The moment of truth, Lori and i have cut and blow dried our models to the requested " Lioness Mane " Lori's model Beth, is blessed with naturally curly auburn hair, she circles the room tossing it rhythmically about her shoulders, there is absolute silence, Lori looks at me and mouths " What did i do wrong ? " before i can say anything, Bedlam ensues ! they all descend on Beth, screaming with enthusiasm, one and all run their fingers through Beth's hair and implore her to keep shaking her head, Kit, my model, met the same fate, her hair had been one very long, ebony black, same length style, Kit vigorously tossed long layered tresses as she went from group to group of exhuberent sorority sisters. Before the seminar ended, we both cut and blow dried five "Lioness Manes" the reaction

to the result of each was beyond our wildest expectations. Mrs. Higgs has come from her office to see what all the noise is about, she too is astounded to see the enthusiasm displayed. She again asks us to come to her office on our way out.

Ruby thanks us again hugs us both and says goodnight, Mrs. Higgs is waiting in her office, we enter and she invites us to take a seat. She smiles and says, " I have never seen such enthusiasm, the girls loved the transformations, what can i do for you ? " she asks, " I noticed you have a bulletin board, perhaps we could leave our business card with you ? " " I would be happy to put it up for you " we shake hands at the doorway and say goodnight, on the drive back to Ocean Bay, Lori says, "Do you think we will get clients from the sorority ? " " I hope so " i reply.

COMMENT

The "Lioness Mane" became the first iconic style for the 70s, California was the epicenter of hair design, and set the standard for the world. The obstreperous " Flower Children " were wilting.
Three years sped by. In 1974, Lori and I took the big step, no, we didn't get married, it was something even more frightening !
We opened our own salon. The following eighteen years were a rocket ride !

THE SUNSHINE FACTORY

Lori and i searched San Diego for the right location, La Jolla was our first choice, but it was too pricey. Lori and i, both rented apartments on Ocean Beach, which was the last stand for the Hippies and Flower children, rising property prices were pushing them ever further south.

One sunny morning, on my run, i noticed a new construction at the end of Ocean Beach Boulevard, the building was a two storey rustic design, with a rough wooden exterior, which blended harmoniously with Ocean Beach pier, only a public parking lot stood between the building and the beach. The next day, i drove to the site to enquire about the availability of rental space. Parking in front of the building, i approach a group of 'Hard Hats' and ask how i can find the developer, one very large member of the group steps forward and says " That would be me, what are you looking for ? " I explained that my partner and i were looking to re locate and would be interested in space to open a beauty salon. " We only have space available on the second floor, and our partners feel it should be offices, not retail. " " Look at it this way, our client flow will bring potential business for everyone." i say, he tells me his name is Don, and shakes my hand, i tell him that will be easy to remember as it's my name too. " Come by this time tomorrow, and I'll have an answer for you. " As I turn to walk to my car, he asks " What make is that ? " " De Tomasao Pantera i tell him, " " Expensive ? " " Very ! "

OCEAN BEACH PROFILE

81

Pool Halls, Beer Bars, a Halfway house, for junkies, Restaurant, Shops, one Movie Theatre, one Bank and an assortment of small business, all desperately in need of renovation. This, was the ambience of Ocean Beach, not a prosperous atmosphere in which to open a 'High End' salon. On the positive side, Ocean Beach was blessed with the largest and newest pier south of Santa Monica. The next day, after a sleepless night, i park in front of the building and again approach the group of 'Hard Hats' i ask for Don, and they tell me he is on the second floor, and to go on up. Reaching the second floor, I find there is a landing that stretches along the outside of the entire floor, there are no inside hallways. Don is talking to an architect, we say hello, he introduces me to Jeff, who designed the building, and says " I thought you and Jeff should get together to discuss what you need " " Does this mean I get space here ? " " Yes " he says and shakes my hand. We walk about 20 feet along the landing and enter a doorway, the space is about 35' wide by 40' deep, windows on two sides which extend from the ceiling to three feet above the floor, I turn to face the ocean, it is un believable ! the pier slices into the ocean to a one point perspective, it reminds me of a Salvador Dali painting. The next evening, Lori and I explore the interior and debate décor.

82

What to name the place? All day we have been suggesting and discounting names, we did not want a 'traditional' beauty salon name, the sun was setting, the surfers and the beach people had all come to a standstill, no one dared to offend this majestic moment. About five minutes later, the sun dipped below the horizon, the sun worshipers clapped in ecstasy. We had our name . . . .
" The Sunshine Factory"
Client : Roberta, is an interior designer, she offered her help in selecting the décor, we followed her advice to the letter, antique wood furniture, plants overflowing with an abundance of green.

NOTE : A write up taken from " Sentinel " a beach newspaper.

"The old line beauty salon is dead ! more or less, women are dropping their weekly 'Baking' sessions under crematory hairdryers, in favor of easy to care for hair, The Sunshine Factory, on Ocean Beach is an innovative idea in today's salons, Don Davis, co-owner, explained, 'The emphasis is toward healthy hair.' Ms. Morango, said, those who come in the late afternoon get to watch the magnificent sunset free."

We opened with just the two of us plus assistants, before we left, we had expanded to an adjoining space and had a staff of thirty ! Lori and i , vastly exceeded our wildest expectations.
Thanks to the write up, we were getting calls from stylists who were interested in the new concept in service. We got lucky.
Two months after opening, stylist Caroline, fresh from the east coast, called for an interview, she was 5' 8" Rubin-esque blonde, with an infectious personality, she was always the first to disrobe, and run into the ocean at our Sunshine Factory, beach parties.
More about these in later chapters !
The second bit of luck, Richard, who was from northern California, was seeking a change in lifestyle after a difficult divorce. Roger, from somewhere in the south (he was always vague about his roots) they were a diverse bunch, but what they had in common made them invaluable to The Sunshine Factory. All three were veteran stylists and had had some degree of training in the new method. So there we were, within the first two months, we had a highly skilled staff.

Client : Ruby. 1:30 P.M. Saturday
Ruby is in for a trim and has brought a sorority sister with her, my assistant is shampooing her. Ruby and i are talking about a party we are invited to, she is concerned her selection of apparel may not be appropriate. " What did you bring ? " i ask " The little black crepe off the shoulder dress " " You will be the sensation of the night " i tell her. " Don, the girl with me is Patty, her boyfriend is in pre-med. His father is a doctor and they are having a running battle over his hair. " " What is wrong with it. " i ask, Ruby says " It is Hippie long . . " but before i can ask any more questions, Patty is escorted to my second chair. Ruby introduces us, " Do you remember talking to me at the demo ? " Patty asks, " How could i forget a beautiful girl. " i reply, " O.K., what was i wearing ? " " A U.C. S.D. sweat shirt, flip flops and very little else " she smiles and says " You

are right about the very little else. " Ruby and i both laugh. We decide on a long 'Lioness mane'.

Hair is like fingerprints always individually different. Patty says, " Don, my boyfriend, Phil, is going to make an appointment with you, to be honest, when his fraternity brothers heard he was going to a beauty salon, they told him to be careful. " About what ? " i ask " You know they think hairdressers are Gay. " " What did you tell him about me ? " " Nothing, but Ruby did. " " What did she say ? " i ask, Ruby , who was in the next chair being blow dried and listening in on our conversation, blurted out " I told him i was fucking you." not realizing that the noise from the drier causes you to raise your voice, the salon went dead quiet for a minute, then Mrs. Butler, a woman in her sixties, said very loudly " Way to go girl ! " with that, the clients and staff break out in hysterical laughter. Ruby says, " Oh my god ! " and joins in, Just another normal day in the salon ! Two weeks later, Saturday 7:00 P.M. last client of the day. Phil has come in by himself, he obviously did not want his fraternity brothers knowing he was having his hair styled. Jeanna, my assistant is California girl, drop dead gorgeous, this has a calming effect on Bi-pedal, testosterone fueled life forms, Jeanna, having performed the ritual of shampooing and conditioning, leads Phil by the hand to my chair, we shake hands. " O.K. tell me about yourself, it will give me an idea as to what style to go for" " This is my senior year, I am in pre med. My father is a doctor in Beverly hills, he wants me to do something 'professional' looking with my hair, and I know it's time to hang up the Flower Power look, what do you suggest ? " " You're right, the below the shoulder look has become passé, why don't we layer it and cut it to just below your ears ? " " Go for it " he says. Thirty minutes later, there is a new Phil looking at himself in the mirror , he is speechless, " You'll get used to it. " I tell him " No, it's great, i can't believe it's me ! " I have to keep him from leaving, as Patty has planned a surprise for him, she has made an arrangement with the restaurant downstairs to chill a bottle of Dom Perignon. When she entered the salon, she made a show of not recognizing Phil and asks me where he is. He laughs and asks, " How do you like the new me ? " she produces the Champagne from behind her back saying, " Phil, you look beautiful " my assistant brings glasses, Phil opens the bottle and pours us a glass each. We toast the 'New' Phil. i am now his new, old, friend. " If i can do anything for you, just ask. " " Well actually, there is something, would your

fraternity be open to the idea of a presentation ? " " Consider it
done. " he says, Patty hugs me, and they leave, very much in love.
NOTE : Phil becomes a plastic surgeon, marries Patty, and they have two
children.
Client : Leslie. Tuesday. 11:30 A.M.
Leslie is a University of San Diego psychology major, this is her third
time at the Sunshine Factory, she is petite, 5' 3" slender with
intelligent, black, radiant eyes. " Don, i have a surprise for you. "
she presents me with a medium sized bag. " Should i try to guess
what it is ? " " No " she says, " Just open it, you will like them "
shaking the bag, it sounds interesting, i unfold the top, and am
immediately assailed with a wonderful aroma, that takes me back to
my childhood, and my grandmothers oatmeal cookies. Reaching in, i
pull out a large oatmeal and raisin cookie, i take a bite, it is
fantastic ! " Where on earth did you buy these ? " i ask " I didn't, i
baked them in the dorm's kitchen " "Very impressive ! you are
beautiful, have great hair, bake wonderful cookies, what else could
anyone want ? "

Leslie decides to go for long, layered and straight, this was a big
step, prior to this, she always requested that the end be trimmed.
NOTE : Usually when a client drastically changes their style, cut, color or
has a perm, it goes hand in hand with a change of lifestyle or 'significant
other.'
Leslie's cut is anew, and i am blow drying it, she is looking in the
mirror, transfixed by the emergence of a new self ." You look great "
i tell her, she smiles, " Thanks Don, i needed to hear that. Can I ask
you a question ? " " Sure " i say " This is embarrassing, but here
goes, i have a problem with my boyfriend, we have been dating for a
year, my sex life is dull, maybe it's my fault, John is the third
boyfriend i've had sex with, the other two were in high school, and
we didn't really know what we were doing, do you have any
suggestions ? "

"Yes, many Clients tell me similar stories, women of all ages, married or single, here is my suggestion, change the atmosphere, you are a nice girl, in the bedroom, be a naughty one, play soft music, instrumentals, use candlelight the flickering softens the skin tone, be super clean, use fragrant soap and body lotion. Take a girlfriend to " Victoria's Secret" and don't be modest, pretend you are models, get each others opinion of what looks sexy, it will be fun" She looks down, not saying anything,
" Is there something else? " i ask, " Yes " she says," i have never had an orgasm " " Leslie, let me ask you some questions, you have had sex education classes, you must surely have covered sexual dysfunctions?"
"Yes" she says, " But we don't discuss our personal problems, besides, i would be too embarrassed to present my problem to the class and i feel comfortable talking to you" " Alright, tell me what you don't do"
" Why ? " she says, " Good question, you know what does not work, so what you don't do, might work for you." After a moment she says "
" You could be right, i perform oral sex on him, but he does not return the favor." " Does he say why not ? " i ask " He tells me the hair gets between his teeth, who wants a mouth full of hair and it's not hygienic"
NOTE : " Victoria's Secret", super models now obviously shave or wax their pubic hair and some women use laser treatment to permanently remove unwanted hair. All this is covered in later chapters.
" Leslie " i say, " Have you ever thought of trimming your pubes? "
" No" she says, " The sixties are over, girls shave their legs and underarms" " How do i do it ? " she asks. " Why don't you make it a joint project between you and your boyfriend "

We have finished the blow out, she vigorously shakes her head, looks in the mirror and says " I love it. " I thank her again for the cookies and wish her luck.
Three days later, Peggy, the receptionist calls me to the front desk, " You have a phone call" she says " I'm sorry but she was insistent" and hands me the phone." Hello" i say, " Don, it's Leslie, sorry to disturb you but i just HAD to tell you, IT WORKED ! he performed oral sex on me. i'm twenty years old, and i've just had my first orgasm ! GOD ! what have i been missing ! i am thinking of becoming a sex therapist."
NOTE she was my client for the next two years, upon graduation, she pursued a career as a sex therapist, helping dysfunctional couples.

COMMENT

Men were apprehensive about having their hair layered, this a new concept for men, the Masters & Johnson study on human sexuality was fifteen years old. It is a tragedy that we are learning so much about the Cosmos but are still unable to gaunter the fundamental need, human sexuality.

SHAMPOO
(The movie)

I remember well , the first time i was made aware of the movie "Shampoo" my five o'clock Friday appointment, Thelma, she was a sweet grandmother, a "hip" 60 something, she had been referred by her granddaughter, Thelma was now a client of three years, a retired school teacher who often told me in candid conversations how delighted she was to see the freedom women had accomplished, especially the freedom to explore their sexuality.

Client: Thelma, 5:00 P.M.

She has been shampooed and is nervously waiting in my chair, i did not see her come in, as most Fridays were, it was a frantic day and i was taking a much needed break in the back room, my assistant, Sharon, informed me Thelma was waiting and she seemed rather excited. As i approached my station, Thelma, with a big mischievous smile on her face, said " Don, i have something to tell you and a few questions, Have you seen the movie " Shampoo" , with Warren Beatty ? " " No" i said, " What is it about ?" (pregnant pause) she continues " You really don't know?" " No" i say " is it good ?" " Don" she says " It's you !, he wears a leather jacket like yours, a silver Concho belt and boots," " Is it a Western? " i ask, " No dummy ! " she says " He's a Beverly Hills hairdresser ! " a pedestrian " Wow" is all i can think to say. "Don" she continues, " Warren is beautiful, but he does not compare to you ! "

" Thelma, Warren is the top male star in Hollywood " " I know, but he is portraying YOU ! " Thelma, i love you, i wish all my clients were so devoted." She says " Wait 'til you see it ! " " What's so special about it ?" i ask " Don, as you are aware, in the movies and T.V. male hairdressers are always depicted as gay, not this time, Warren is pursued by every woman in Beverly Hills, and he services all of them !

i don't know how to answer this, " Enlighten me" i say "I'm certain this
will be of benefit to you" " I believe you Thelma, now, to something
really important, the brown bag on the counter emanating that
intoxicating aroma, possibly your famous "Toll House" cookies? "
"Yes" she laughs, " And they are for you."
Sharon, who has been listening to our conversation tells Thelma a girl
friend called her last night asking if she had seen " Shampoo" I asked "
Who was the friend and what was her impression ?" "Don" she replies,
 " The same as Thelma, she said Warren's character described you and
you know Wanda, my friend, i use her as a model for the hair cutting

classes. " Well, this seems interesting, maybe i will see the movie"
Thelma says " This is not a case of maybe, Don, you HAVE to see it !
Pat who, as you know is my granddaughter, took me along with two
of her friends, driving back, all three were in a heightened state
of arousal, all they could talk about was how sexy Warren's
character George, was and how they would like to meet him, Pat
kept insisting they should come with her next week when she gets
her hair cut." Finishing Thelma's cut and blow dry, i again thank
her for the cookies and the movie review Thelma wishes me an
enigmatic "Good luck"
There were five stylists taking a break in the back room, passing the
cookies round, i ask if anyone has heard about the movie
"Shampoo" Caroline and Richard said yes, the others said no,
Caroline said one of her clients told her the main character
resembled Don, Richard added that two of his clients asked him if
the movie was anything like real life, but since i have not seen it,
i told them i could not comment.

Next day, there is a buzz in the salon, almost everyone's clients are
asking their stylist if they have seen "Shampoo" and by midday,
five of my clients have informed me that i MUST see the film.
Client: Kelly: 1:30 P.M.
She is a slender thirty something, she is in my chair and we are
discussing changing her style for a shorter, more care free low
maintenance look. Half way into the procedure, she says " Don,
my husband and i saw "Shampoo" Tuesday night, i told him,
Warren has captured your persona, Bill thought that was
interesting and wants to know if he could have an appointment for
a style change" " Sure" i say, " Tell him to call "

NOTE: Bill was to be my first male client as a direst result of the movie.
Kelly says " Bill has great hair, it's a little wavy and he wants to learn
how to blow dry it" " Don't worry i'll be happy to show him how to
do it." Kelly is looking in the mirror. " This is what i wanted " she
says, running her fingers through much shorter hair, "No reason
to blow it , kind'a spikey, looks like an un made bed."
"You look Hot" i say " Don, i would like to ask you something personal"
" No problem" i say " Several of my girl friends are your clients, three
of us were discussing the movie at lunch, three glasses of wine

later, i was chosen to ask you if you have sex with your clients,
like Warren in the movie ? " " Kelly, my lips are sealed, i never
betray a confidence." she says, " You just answered my question.
My friends want to invite you to dinner." " Tell your mysterious
friends to ask" " No Don" she says " They mean to gather." "
Are you serious ?" i ask " Yes " she says " Are you going to tell
me who they are ? " " No." she says, " They will tell you when
they get their hair cut ".
It was a very busy Saturday, to say "Shampoo" was the main topic is an
understatement !
My last client, Yoshia, is Japanese, she is my girlfriend, we met at
Barbizon, she was enrolled in a modeling class and i was teaching
the importance of hair design, she was incredibly beautiful, if she
had been three inches taller, she would have been the worlds first
Japanese supermodel. We finish with the blow dry at seven, her
hair is midnight blue / black and long enough to almost sit on, the
Japanese have the most luxuriant hair in the world.
" Don" she says," I called your friend's dates, we have a surprise for
you, we are going to meet in Fashion Valley." Note : a brief
history, my two friends, i will call them Tom and Jerry, are successful
real estate agents, and are Sunshine Factory clients.

We meet in front of the multiplex theatre in Fashion Valley, the
surprise is obvious, we are going to see " Shampoo" it is a sell out
but Yoshida has paid the usher to reserve six seats together, the
lights dim, There is George, on a motorcycle going like hell
through Hollywood, for the next two hours, i am spellbound ! the
movie portrayed my profession in complete candor. Afterwards,
and amid much kidding from all, we decide to go to Tom and
Jerry's condos on South Mission, we meet in Jerry's condo, Tom

and his date, having arrived before us, have two ice buckets of Dom Perignon waiting. Over the next ten years, we contributed greatly to the success of the brand in San Diego. Joan asks me how I liked the movie, " What can i say " This is sensory overload, hairdressers have never been depicted in this heterosexual way before. Example, Johnny Carson always made jokes about Gay hairdressers. Trish, Jerry's date, asks " Do you have sex with your clients ?" Yoshida interrupts, " Don never asks his clients for dates, after Don's seminar at Barbizon, i called for an appointment, we got along well, he cut my hair, and showed me how I could make quick changes for my photo album, on my second appointment i requested the receptionist to make me his last client of the day. it was a Tuesday night, so thinking Don might not have any plans, interrupting, i say " You had plans! " " Be quiet " Yoshida says\, " This is my tale, no pun intended, so when Don finished with my hair, i asked him if he would like to have a glass of wine, he said that's a good idea, and did i have a preference, a favorite bar ? i said yes, how about your place.

Jerry says " It's time to open another bottle " Trish stands up and says " While you boys are performing your task, the ladies will retire to the bedroom to prepare your surprise " After they had left, Tom asks " Do either of you have any idea what might be in the box Joan brought in ? " Jerry said no and i said " I don't know either , but whatever it is i'm sure we will enjoy it" Another glass of Champagne each and much car talk. The girls are back, all three are wrapped in towels, Joan is holding the mysterious box, she says " Ready or not, here is the surprise, on cue, they whip off the towels, yes, they are totally naked, three very different women, each incredibly gorgeous in their own way, Yoshida, ivory skin small breasts, delicate bone structure, shaved pubes and black hair piled on top of her head, held in place with six red chopsticks if she had lived in an earlier century she would have been Geisha. Trish with her natural red wavy hair with golden highlights shining in the light, pubes trimmed to the shape of a red Valentine, slightly freckled white alabaster skin resembling an Irish fairy goddess . Joan, California surfer girl, chiseled muscle structure, long layered sun streaked hair framing a Patrician sculptured face, green cat like eyes, perfect white teeth, full lips, sun lotion commercial quality, tanned skin. She is holding the mystery box waist high, bikini line waxed pubes, she is a natural blonde. Joan begins to take bottles and brushes from the box saying," Remember the party scene in the movie ? some of the people were body painting each other, get your clothes off, you guys aren't shy are you ? " needless to say, we stripped off in an instant. None of the great masters ever put brush to canvas with more inspiration than we did. Three hours and more corks popped we, had showered en mass, Tom and Jerry's shower room could easily accommodate ten people. The night ended with six satiated people in a Jacuzzi on Jerry's roof beneath a starlit Californian night sky, on the drive back to my place, Yoshida told me the girls had decided they would like to swap partners at the next party she wanted to know if we guys had a problem with that, I told her no problem.

During the next three months, Tom, Jerry and i christened our parties " Jacuzzi Nights"

UNISEX ?

The profession has now become "Unisex" the first time i saw this on the cover of "Vogue" Magazine, i thought it sounded like a third sex ! with the influx of men, i am beginning to hear men talk candidly about their sex lives. (In recent times it has become fashionable for celebrities on "Fox News" channel to openly discuss their sexually dysfunctional relationships, "My Space" blogs and chat rooms serve the same purpose for non celebrities) Before "The Net." beauty salons served this purpose, the advantage, real people talking in real time.

Stay tuned, the temperature will soar in the next chapters !

THE CONTEST

The stylists have decided to have a contest, each one puts ten Dollars in the " pot ", not counting me and Lori, there are twenty five staff, grand total wagered, two hundred and fifty Dollars ! factor in inflation, that would be close on one thousand in today's money. Contest rules. On their honor, they will keep a score of the clients they have sex with, they are not allowed to solicit sex, the clients must not be aware of the contest, and must be the instigators of the liaison, the guys are convinced this is unfair, you don't have to be a rocket scientist to realize the girls are odds on to win, or so you would think ! ! ! !

The highest scoring girl for the month was Dottie, (a big busted blonde who often stripped at parties) scored fifteen, and the winner . .
. . . Phil, a good looking ex-bartender, his score . . . twenty ! Women have reached equality, at least in the bedroom. The down side of this, was for the stylists who were in relationships, when the contest became known, their partners were more than a bit miffed to say the least !

Client Paula : 2 : 00 P.M.

She is a " Transplanted New Yorker " , living in California for the past five years, she has ' gone native ' . Paula is having a bi-monthly, sun streaking touch up. " Don " she says, " Is it true what the shampoo girl told me." " Probably not, what did she tell you ? "
" She told me there is a contest to see which stylist will have the most sexual encounters with their clients, is it true that the clients must ask ? " " Yes that is the basic rule" " Don " she says, " Are you in the contest ? " " No " i tell her, " That's no fun. " she says, " I wanted to volunteer. Patty is my husband's stylist, do you know if he was a volunteer ? "
" No" i say, " I do not want to be involved in their contest " she smiles and says " Could i tempt you ? " " Never say no to a beautiful lady." An hour later, freshly sun streaked, having paid the receptionist, she returns to me, slips her hand in my pocket and whispers, " I have checked your schedule, meet me at eight, the " O.B." bar"

Checking my pocket i find she has left a generous gratuity of fifty Dollars. The O.B. bar is on the second floor, overlooking the pier, there is a good surf today and the surfers daringly dart between the pilings, you don't have to be crazy to be a surfer, but it helps. Paula has not arrived, joining some of the local O.B, 'ites, we are extolling the joys of another day in paradise as the sun begins it's slow, magnificent plunge below the horizon. One of my companions nudges me and says " A goddess has just entered ! " turning to evaluate the truth in his statement, a 5' 9" vision in an off the shoulder, light yellow linen, full skirted, semi transparent dress, tightly belted at the waist, with a red silk sash, is gliding towards me. Paula has brought a hush to the room, she reaches out, takes my hand, pulling me towards her, i am engulfed in an intoxicating fragrance, a blend of her natural aroma and her perfume, her lips lightly caress mine. The room breaks out in enthusiastic cheers and applause, one and all we turn to watch the sun depart in magnificence. We go to a corner table and order two glasses of white wine, " Don " Paula says, " I have an open marriage but i am a little nervous" " Don't be shy, you have shared a confidence with me for two years." " You are right, you know more about me than my husband ! "

Finishing the wine, Paula says she will follow in her car.

 It is less than a mile to my cottage, perched on the edge of a thirty foot cliff, if you listen with an open mind, the purity of a Beethoven sonata is heard in the breaking of the waves, a spiritual fulfillment to the end of the day. Soft Jazz is playing on the sound system, Paula is standing on my polar bear rug, slowly, she disrobes, her dress slides to her waist, revealing perfect shaped breasts, unfettered by a bra, bending forwards slightly, she pushes soft linen folds over rounded hips gliding down two endless legs, the dress surrounds her ankles as though reluctant to abandon perfection. She steps back and with a practiced movement, flicks the dress with the motion of a slender foot, floating gently, the yellow linen dress comes to rest next to me on the couch, i clap with joy, this is a woman knowing who she is, at the apogee of her power, she is un ashamedly naked. " Don " she says, " I have a request before we enjoy the night, will you trim my pubes in a heart shape ? "

NOTE : this was not an unusual request, a prominent ladies fashion magazine had published a pictorial of various "pubic" designs, clients were asking how to achieve these results. It was a night of magical splendor, as we kissed goodnight, Paula told me five of her friends who were my clients, knew of the contest and intended to let me know of their interest.

BRIEF SUMMARY

Example, The Shampoo Effect.
The Michael Jordan Effect is studied in economic classes in universities. When capital growth reaches phenomenal levels, economists are compelled to quantify it.

Reasons, The Jordan Effect can be applied to local constructs as well as international models.
Why is this valuable ? it is a tool that allows product marketing firms, specializing in predicting sales potentialities. Advise their clients in sales strategies. The overall benefit when the mathematical formula has been proven, it can be applied to totally unrelated events with precise detriments.

THE SHAMPOO EFFECT

The Warren Beattie movie about a Beverly Hills hairdresser, within one month, changed the dynamics of an entire industry. NOTE this could be a separate study in the theory of un intended consequence. Shampoo, the movie, made it acceptable for men to patronize beauty salons.
The effect / consequence –
It increased the wealth of an industry by a value of 50% in an incredibly short time frame. I challenge the great laureates of economics to find another example of where this unprecedented level of growth occurred, without any injection of capital or any additional employment of labor. In simpler terms, the Shampoo Effect was a sociological and economic anomaly.

THE FARA PHENOMENON

Fara Fawcet did not make her hair style famous, her hairstyle made HER famous ! The " Fara " as it was labeled, by stylists could be adapted to almost any female, Clients brought in the poster of her in the one piece, red bathing suit, demanding to have her hairstyle. This was the epitome of the California girl that every guy in the world was fantasizing over, this brave photo expressed the resilience that is uniquely American. If you study history, using fashion as a guide, you can predict the general feeling of an era, whether constricted of liberal, simply by observing hair styles and couture.
In the mid seventies, protests and political tension decreased. A time of much needed rejoicing and re evaluation was sweeping the land, In the last five years of the decade, women have reaped   savored the fruition of what their mothers and older sisters had struggled

so hard to achieve. This is possibly the greatest social legacy ever bequeathed to a new generation.

SAN DIEGO NIGHTS

Client : Herman 1:30 P.M. Tuesday

Herman is a client of four years, he was introduced to me by his then, girlfriend, he was in his last year of law school, since passing the Bar exam, he is San Diego's leading product liability lawyer. While cutting his hair, we are discussing the merits of various marques of fast cars, oddly, cars and not women were the topic most articulated with male clients. NOTE : Probably has something to do with "Boys and their Toys" He invites me to a party on Friday night at his house, he says " Bring someone if you want but it's not required "   " Why not ? " i ask, " Because the party will be an adventure and will be more spontaneous if guests come, un attached. " Sounds interesting, but i have a commitment, this is our first date, she is a client of two years, and recently divorced she is quite liberal" " Good " he says " Bring her, Don" he adds, i have one request, please bring the Ferrari, you will have a parking space reserved in front of the house, there will be parking attendants so the car will be safe i can assure you." After thinking for a moment, i Say " O.K."

Friday night, Party time !

Joan arrives 8:00 o'clock at my house, meeting her with a long stemmed red rose in one hand and a glass of champagne in the other, Joan enters with a flourish, accepting the offering, she lightly kisses me on both cheeks. A vision, Fara Fawcet blonde streaked tresses, a little black dress Coco Chanel would have envied ! her fragrance, subtle and intoxicating. Sipping Champagne from her glass gives me a minute to enjoy the magnetism this female exudes. Regaining my equilibrium, i ask " Did you have trouble finding my house ? " " No " she says, "A friend lives in the neighborhood, she gave me good directions, Marta, said she is dying to see your house, had to promise to tell you she wants to be invited to a Jacuzzi party" " How did she know i have a Jacuzzi ?" she says, " some of her friends are Sunshine Factory clients, their stylists described a staff Christmas party tell her to make

an appointment," Joan says " Good idea, now tell me who designed your house, and this fireplace ! i have never seen anything like it ! " I tell her " The fireplace is a replica of one from a restaurant in Hollywood i used to frequent, it's what my interior designer refers to as a " Conversation pit."
The night is cool, a hypnotic fire blazes in the hearth, soft jazz is playing from concealed speakers arranged throughout the house. NOTE : the fireplace is three and a half feet below the common floor, you go down three steps, the fire pit is square, five feet to the side, finished in black slate, two and a half feet high, a top ledge one foot in width, also covered in black slate, the interior wall is six inch concrete block, the pit's interior has a gas system fed into six hundred pounds of sand from the Sahara dessert, the gas rises through the sand to the surface , the result is a shimmering flame that moves across the sand, three sides of the pit have built in couches, the open side is glassed to a height of thirty five feet by thirty feet wide, the fire is vented by a round funnel five feet in diameter with a thirty five foot high chimney all made from metal and attached to the ceiling by four chains all painted black. The conversation pit overlooks decking, a garden and Jacuzzi, surrounded by a ten foot wall, total privacy. All in all, one of my better ideas.
Finishing the Champagne, we exit through the kitchen, turning the garage light on, Joan exclaims " What is that ! ? " " Which one ? " I ask, "The yellow one " she says, the "yellow one", as she calls it, is a 1936 supercharged Cord Phaeton, 100% restored. " It's fantastic !" she says, " Can we drive it to the party ? " " No, our host has requested me to bring the Ferrari."
NOTE: It is a 365 G.T.S. Daytona, Cruising up 405 towards La Jolla, Joan asks " How fast will it go ? " " On the way to Las Vegas, 170 on the speedometer." " Could we go faster ?" she asks, " NO, the police have a tendency to notice bright red cars, besides, our turn off is coming up" La Jolla village drive takes us to La Jolla shore's drive. Herman's house sits on a high cliff, overlooking the ocean, true to his word, there is a parking space in front of his house, the valet directs me to park between two Ferrari Testarossas. This is going to be a good party, i hit the buzzer, the door is opened by a girl in a French maid's outfit, introducing myself and Joan, she checks in a book, smiles, and asks us to

follow her, as she turns to lead us to the festivities, Joan and I laugh, the dress has no back, a white lace collar, black bodice and apron tied at the back she is nude from her neck to her garter belt, black fishnet hose, and four inch black stiletto heels. We dutifully follow her to the small beach cottage, which is what Herman refers to it as, Actually, it is 8,000 Sq feet, our destination, the pool area, the Jacuzzi and pool are filled with frolicking Nature Worshippers, in other words, they were naked. A long table set with the specialties from La Jolla's four star restaurants. Tom And Jerry, having donned swimming trunks, are talking to a six foot, drop dead gorgeous black girl and her diminutive Asian girl friend, i guide Joan over to my friends, and perform the formalities, the black girl, Venus, asks Joan if she would like to change into what they are wearing, Joan smiles and says " Sure, let's do it" they depart with Joan in the middle.

108

NOTE : the costume is Hawaiian "Lava Lava" , not to be mistaken for the more modest Sarong, it consists of a brief "Hip Hugger", flower print, tied at the hip, extending diagonally across, and barely covering, the "Mons of Venus" , to just above the knee of the opposite leg, no top, the breasts are covered with multiple lays of fragrant scented flowers.

Conversing with Tom and Jerry, we unanimously agree, we have to improve our parties, spying us, Herman approaches with a glass of Champagne in one hand and his arm round one of my clients, she is dressed in the de'rigeur Hawaiian costume. " Don ! glad to see you," he says, Grace, who is with him, smiles and says " Great party, maybe later your friends and i can get together," Tom and Jerry instantly answer " No problem" Joan has returned, The "Lava Lava" leaves nothing to the imagination !

109

She tells me her new friends are going to show her a party room, "Do you know Grace? " i ask, "No, but i've seen her in the salon" Joan says, they kiss on the cheeks, Grace says " Let's get together later" Joan says, "Sounds Good" As she departs with Africa and Asia, Tom says " Let's go exploring " " O.K. " i say, " But first, i want to change" Herman points me in the direction of the dressing rooms. There is a generous selection of Lava Lavas and Speedo's, i choose a black pair. Returning to find Tom and Jerry have disappeared. It is time to go exploring, before the night is over, I count eight bedrooms, a games room, plus a dance floor. guests are grouped according to kindred spirits, seeking shared pleasures. Entering a dimly lit bedroom a blonde head of hair i recognize is engrossed between two very long black legs, the black girls face is not visible as an Asian girl is sitting on it ! The Asian girl spots me and motions for me to join them, as my motto says "Never say no to a beautiful lady ! " By two A.M., having partaken of the offered pleasures, i return to the pool to find the host in conversation with Tom and Jerry. " What's up guys ?" I enquire, Herman says " We have decided to start a party group, that would take turns in hosting parties at their homes" Jerry says " We will keep it very exclusive " Tom says, " You could let selected clients join the group". Look guys, i NEVER ask a client for a date" Jerry interjects, " Are you serious ! you never ask a client for a date ? " " " That's right" i say but don't worry, there are several Sunshine Factory clients here, i'm certain there will be enquiries about future parties, why don't you discreetly hint there are other parties scheduled ?" Herman says, " Good idea, Tom, Jerry, let's get the rumor started." Sipping Perrier, and observing the freedom displayed by all as they partake of this sexual smorgasbord. NOTE: At neither this, or any other party did I ever see any display of jealousy.   Joan has found me, and takes me by the hand, " Let's go exploring" " Lead on " i reply two hours and three rooms later, we bid adieu to our host. Arriving at my house, Joan kisses me goodbye and says " Keep me in mind for future parties.

I slept for twelve hours and greeted the new day with a gym work out, that was hard ! Just another day in paradise !

COMMENT

The final five years of the 70's San Diego was a party scene second to none ! San Francisco and New York had "Plato's Retreat" and Los Angeles, "Swinger bars." They verged on the frantic, they were more in sync with Las Vegas where it is demanded that you have a good time ! San Diego was the complete opposite, there was harmony in the party scene, you enjoyed yourself (and others!) at you own pace, you never once, felt you were " On stage."

Client : Ginger.

She is a sales person in real estate, a single mother of an eleven year old daughter. A client of three years, she is thirty something, petite, slightly curly shoulder length auburn hair and a spunky personality, often she is compared to Sally Field.

Saturday, Five o'clock. Ginger is my last client of the day, having finished with a trim and blow dry, she is in the dressing room changing, as i was very busy when she arrived and not having seen what she was now wearing, as she approaches, i am speechless, Wrapped like a Christmas package begging to be opened, the ensemble is a near transparent light Jade green off the shoulder gauze wrap dress, belted around a very slim waist by a dark green satin sash, and barely long enough to cover the essentials ! four inch heeled open toed shoes, deep red to match the toe and fingernails, gold chain necklace and gold sleeve bracelets on each slender wrist, a seductive vision, as she slides into my chair, the last mystery is revealed, red silk bikini ! " Don" she says," You don't mind if i use your mirror to apply my make- up do you ?" " No, do what ever you like" " Be careful ! " she says " Maybe i will ! how do you like my dress ?" " What can i say, Words fail me " " Yes" she says " But what do you really think?" "Someone is going to be very lucky tonight " i tell her. "Don" she says, the club i'm going to is private, swear you won't tell anyone and i will tell you about the activities." " My lips are sealed, so what is so special about it ? " " It's a private members club gathering only once a month. at the home of a college professor. "

NOTE: the police, on a tip off from a neighbor (who probably was not invited) raided the private house causing a legal mess, it was in the courts for years. With his wife, they host free parties for carefully screened couples, married and single, there are more or less twenty people, some are faculty members, others, prominent business people.

I ask " What is unique about these parties ?" the house is quite large, four bedrooms, each designed with a different erotic theme, from Harem to Bondage, you make a donation of 100 Dollars, per couple, hors d'eurves, wine, and Champagne are served, no drugs are allowed. This is the good bit, four completely naked co-eds serve the guests, they are heavily tipped, the guests are generous, the Co-Ed's do not take part in the festivities" "Sounds like you are going to have a good time" i tell her, She says "Would you like to be my guest some time? " " Let me think about it " Ginger looks in the mirror, and smiles, " My date is here" she says. Turning around, i see a very tall, stunning, model thin lady in a Chinese Mandarin ankle length black satin dress it is embroidered from Mandarin collar to hem with red dragons, front and back as she walks towards us, a shapely leg is exposed from ankle to waist. The dragon ladies hair is loosely piled on top of her head and held in place by eight chopsticks, arranged in a fan like formation, she looks familiar, then one of the stylists calls her by name, i did not recognize her, but i have spoken to her on several occasions, she glides over to Ginger, says Hi, and hugs her, they spend the next five minutes complimenting each other , saying goodbye, i wish them a good party. The dragon lady comes closer and whispers in my ear, " The next time you cut my husbands hair, be sure to tell him how good i looked" " No problem" i say. A week later, taking a break in the back room, i overhear two stylists talking, Patty is telling June, her sister who is in her third year of college sometimes works parties for one of her professors." is this the party my client went to last week ? you remember, Patty, the dragon lady picked her up " Patty laughs and says "My sister told me those two put on quite a show"!

THE WORLD'S SECOND OLDEST PROFESSION

Sex workers : Every city i have worked in, from Evansville Indiana, Beverly Hills, San Diego, Miami, New York, New York. Sex workers have been part of my clientele, and like other clients, they tell their hairdressers everything.

Client : Dorothy

Dorothy has been one of my more lucrative clients for the best part of a year, on her first appointment she un-abashedly told me she was a high priced courtesan, the epitome of a Californian goddess, golden blonde hair cascading to the middle of her back, 5' 9" perfectly sculpted body, the result of a five day a week, gym regime with a personal trainer. She was very intelligent, the holder of a degree in political science from one of California's most prestigious universities. Often, she told me who her clients were, and their sexual preferences, her client list read like the society page. NOTE : Several high priced escorts and Madams, have published their memoirs. What follows is a history of one of her clients, and all the gory details, as told to me. It is in the public domain, having been sensualized in San Diego (4th estate) you only have to check the archives to verify.

8:30 P.M. Friday.

Client : Dorothy

A warm San Diego sunset is performing as scripted, the entire salon has paused to watch wonder of nature.

Dorothy is sitting in my chair, we have both remained silent as the sun descends below the horizon, perhaps it was the spirituality of the moment, that evoked her catharsis. She is not in her usual mode of behavior, so i enquire " Is something wrong with your hair ? " " No, no " she says, " Don have you been reading in the paper recently about the Judge who was caught charging sexual services to his credit card ? " "Yes " i tell her,

" Clients are commenting on how dumb he was to use his card in the first place ! " Dorothy continues, " What makes it really newsworthy is that the card was also run through a very famous restaurant "

NOTE : The restaurant was investigated for Mob connections. "And the nature of the sex acts ? " i ask, "Is it true as reported by the press ? " " Yes ", she says " He wanted me to perform the " Golden Blessing " on him, he lay nude in the bath, and i would urinate on his face."

" Wasn't that messy ? " " No she replies, " he held a sheet of plastic over his face." NOTE : this act was unheard of by the general public in the 70s XXX movies now feature this rarity. Progress sinks lower !

Dorothy introduced her working colleagues to the salon, some were my clients and some used other stylists, always after one of them had had an appointment, the back room would be a' buzz with what had been disclosed, comparing notes, they were often astounded by the sexual acts described, most of which they were previously, blissfully un aware of ! NOTE : Internet porn has sadly left nothing to the imagination .

These services ranged from the bizarre to comical. Bear in mind the clients of these ladies, were the business and political elite of San Diego. In the 70s these good citizens were not exclusive to one sex, both men and women used their services.

THE ENTERPRISING HAIRDRESSER

Richard, one of our male stylists, frequented massage parlors, as it turned out, Richard benefited economically from his hobby, in the period of one year, he told me he had added one hundred clients to his client base, massage parlor girls all. i asked him how it was possible that he had used the services of that many girls, after some embarrassed hesitation, he said he posted the Sunshine Factory flier on their notice board, i laughed and told him, since the business was legal in San Diego it showed good initiative. They charged less than their fashion Valley sisters, but made up for it by sheer numbers. NOTE : I was told this by a client.

COMMENTS

Why do i say sex workers is the second oldest profession ? Simple, before they went out onto the streets of Babylon, Thebes, Athens, Rome, they had their hair done, nails painted and make up applied, yes, they went to the beauty salon !

The San Diego massage parlors were not to last, the keepers of public morality ordered a crack down, the vice squad officers, passing themselves off as " Johns " paid for services, with humorous results In order to arrest the girls, they had to penetrate, vaginally, anally or have oral sex performed on them ! consequently, San Diego's most excellent investigative news reporters, covering the court proceedings, publicized the devotion to duty of San Diego's finest ! The ensuing scandal set grounds for divorces, oddly enough, the police department, in their wisdom, reasoned that married officers would be better qualified for this line of work ! !

I almost meet Paul Mitchell

Deciding it is time to seek out new innovations, in cutting hair, my first choice is Paul Mitchell hair cutting club New York, New York as he is top of the pecking order.

The academy is in Manhattan, remembering the movie " The Way We Were" (Robert Redford and Barbara Streisand) the Plaza hotel was my choice, unfortunately, this was before Donald Trump owned it, sold it, owned it . . . . Motel 8 would have been better ! the up side was that I could walk to the academy.

The vicissitudes of fate. The first day, the class is informed that Paul has sold the hair cutting club to Glenby and now resides in a trailer on a beach in Hawaii. The week sped by, friendships made, knowledge assimilated and vows to keep in contact made.

Friday, the last day, a farewell party in an Italian restaurant, Greenwich Village, the food, New York, at it's best. My class mates and i all vowed to take our newly acquired knowledge to our prospective salons and share it with our fellow stylists. With morning flights, we hug each other, one and all and bid each other safe journeys. Having tickets for a Broadway show assures me of two more nights in The Big Apple. Returning to the Plaza, a message awaits, My San Diego clients will pick me up at 10:30 it is 9:30, with an hour to kill, i saunter into the famous " Oak Bar", just off the lobby, Many memorable movie scenes have been shot here, ordering a glass of wine, i tell the bartender to charge it to my room, he tells me it has been taken care of by the two ladies sitting at a table behind me, he tells me they would like me to join them. they are New York, stylish, in their mid to late thirties, Elisabeth owns a Soho art gallery, she is outfitted in a navy blue business suit, complete with white shirt, white on white tie, gold cufflinks, double pleated pants, patent leather black four inch heels, no make up, black hair, military short, jelled and combed straight back, the fragrance, Old Spice. very Marlene Dietrich ! NOTE : Madonna, on occasions, has adopted this style, she calls it Boy Toy. Her companion is elegantly French, resembling Catherine De Neuve, she is dressed in a rose hued sheath, slashed to mid thigh, one leg gracefully crosses the other, a four inch heel stiletto shoe dangles suggestively on rose lacquered toes, thick, long, white blonde hair, hazel, Nefratti slanted eyes heavily outlined with black mascara, pink glossed lips, a simple platinum chain necklace and matching bracelet, her scent, Chanel No 5. This

observation was made during our introductions Lauren asks me if i have plans for the night, if not, they would like me to accompany them to a party, " Sorry " i said , and TRULY meant it ! " But i have a commitment ". Lauren says the invitation is for an unforgettable party. My name is paged, and shaking hands with the ladies, i bid them farewell. Alas, i will always wonder what i missed ! A black Cadillac stretch limo is waiting at the curb. Lionel, one of my San Diego clients, jumps out, shakes my hand and gestures for me to get in. His wife, Esoie, also a client, is sitting on the far side, a glass of Champagne in each hand. " This one is for you." She says, taking the offered libation, we touch glasses, she says " Tonight we party like there is no tomorrow ! " " Esoie, where did you get that dress ? " " A shop on fifth avenue, " she says. Lionel interjects, " It cost me 1,000 Dollars, and she's worth it ! "

" How do you like it ? " she asks. " Ravishing is the only word to describe it." The dress is backless with a halter top that plunges between her breasts to her navel, ankle length blue silk crepe slashed on both sides to her hip, a string of pearls looped around her long graceful neck, four inch, open toed blue snake skin shoes and matching small clutch bag round off the ensemble. Esoie is sitting with slightly parted legs, the front panel of the dress flows between two very long, tanned legs, her scent, Tabu, permeates the air, Lionel tells her " Show Don how you prepared for the party. " " Don " she says, " Remember the last time you did my hair, we were talking about designs for pubes ? well, look what i did " she parts her legs, " How do you like my design ? " she has shaved her pubes. " What can i say, you are all woman ! "

PLATO'S RETREAT

Reaching our destination, there is a line of " The beautiful people " waiting to enter, Loinel says " Don't worry, we are the guests of a permanent member. The people in line are members just for the one night only, admission is limited, four interesting people exit the limo in front of us, Esoie exclaims, That's Mick Jagger and the girl married to the Canadian politician ! She might have been right, the two oriental women were far more interesting. The limo leaves, our driver pulls forward, we 'de-limo' the doorman, who is just a little smaller than " Andrea the giant " smiles as Lionel hands him the invitation and scrutinizing it, says " Welcome to Plato's, enjoy the night."

As we enter, a hostess greets us and asks if we wish to change to robes, Esioe says " Let's change " the hostess rings a chime, a drape is parted, and for a brief moment, i see a dimly lit room with people in various modes of dressing, actually it was hard to notice anything other than the goddess standing in front of me, with heels, she was taller than me, high, pointed breasts, a " flat top " design hair style, glistening ebony skin, powdered in gold dust, shaved and nude, she informed us her name was Gana and she would be our guide. Lionel, and Esoie were as dumbstruck as i was ! Esoie, who was the first to recover, says, " Lead on " Gana turns, parts the drapes and motions us through, we enter the changing room, it is lit by concealed lights, lockers are spaced in rows with padded benches, similar to what you would find in a Y.M.C.A. the difference being, that this changing room is Co-Ed ! Gana tell us we can leave the locker keys with the receptionist after changing, just remember your number. The lockers, we discover, give you a choice of robe, or towel. Party goers can choose towel, robe or nothing, seeing those who have changed. Leaving, the balance is even between robes and nothing, Esoie and Lionel have decide on robes which are very short. The towel will work for me. Esoie smiles and says " Don, i thought you were thin ! " my body , 185 Lbs. no fat. Lionel says " I never told her what you looked like without clothes " NOTE : Lionel was a member of Leo Stern's Gym, same as me.

We leave the lockers, and part company, my first stop is the bar, tired warriors of both sexes are refreshing themselves between partaking of the variety of entertainment offered. The petite, nude, blonde sitting on the barstool next to mine, is asking the distinguished looking man on the other side of her, if he would like to feel her new vagina, with no hesitation, he inserts two fingers and after exploring to his satisfaction, they depart. The bartender brings me my order, a glass of white wine, i ask " What did she mean new vagina ? " he laughs and says " Rachael used to be Richard " " You mean that's a transgender ? " " Yes, Rachael is very popular, never says no ! " he recommended i try her. During the night i observed her with multiple partners, in what was referred to in high school as a "Gang Bang" NOTE : This was a typical teenage fantasy, i never participated in one or knew anyone who had.

123

COMMENTARY

Neighbors either wanted to be invited to my Jacuzzi parties, or wanted me to depart the neighborhood.

365 G.T.S. Daytona Spyder. Dr. Bruce Sand was the original owner, a prominent Beverly Hills eye surgeon, we both wish we had kept it, present value . . . . . . 1,000,000 Dollars

95% of the ladies who attended the Jacuzzi parties were married, or had been.

It is a fact that women dress for other women rather than for men, women have a better eye for color and symmetry.

Women clients often asked me if i had female clients interested in same sex, relations, these were women of all ages and ethnicity.

124

LOVE PASSAGES IN THE SALON

In today's fast paced, high tec. world, people are finding it difficult to interact, the computer, via the internet, has made it mandatory to express ones sexual fantasies in dismal solitude. There is one solution, ask your hairdresser to set aside one night a month as a " Singles only night " and for this special event, they may offer discount on services, hairdressers are intelligent, he or she will see the advantage in offering this service.

LOVE IS IN THE AIR

7:00 P.M. Thursday :   Clients : Barbara and Cheryl
Barbara and Cheryl are manageresses of a popular boutique in Fashion Valley. We are discussing the pro's and con's of changing her hair color, which is light brown, i suggest subtle highlights which would enhance her skin tone, Cheryl agrees, Barbara says " O.K. let's do it " Sorry i say, we will have to do it another time as there is one more client after you both, he is always in a hurry, you will recognize him, he does a lot of T.V. commercials with his dog." " O.K. next time " she says. Twenty minutes into the cut, Cheryl is sitting in the next chair, we have been gossiping about the fashion world, which model is sleeping with which rock star, or the latest Hollywood stud actor. NOTE : Thirty years later, and the same topics are being discussed. Finishing Barbara's cut and blow out, she takes a seat in the waiting area, Cheryl, having been shampooed, my assistant escorts her to my chair, we discuss changing her style, she wants something she can towel dry and fluff it up with her fingers, in other words, low maintenance. NOTE : This was before liquid styling products. " With your natural wave " i tell her, " This will work. " glancing in the mirror, and seeing the receptionist approaching, she seems distraught, reaching my station, she whispers in my ear, " Don, Mr. T is here, thirty minutes early ! what do i do ? " What was to occur next, started a sequence of events which would greatly impact upon the lives of two people, often, i have wondered what if the instructions i had given the receptionist had been different ? " Give Mr. T a seat next to Barbara and give him a cup of coffee." she gently guided Mr. T to a chair. The best script writers in Hollywood could not have come up with anything better than what happened next ! The phone rang, the receptionist excused herself, and returned to

the front desk, this left Mr. T. sitting with a helpless look on his face, Barbara, sensing his discomfort, graciously asked him how he would like his coffee ? " Black " he finally managed to articulate, smiling, Barbara rose, and glided to the coffee caddy, whereupon, she poured a Dixie cup of very black coffee, returning to Mr. T, she bowed her head, and gave him the cup. a Japanese tea ceremony could not have been executed with more grace and beauty !

126

Putting the finishing touches to Cheryl's blow out," Mr. T " i say, are you ready to be shampooed ? " " No hurry " he says, Now this is really weird ! he hasn't said a word to Barbara after thanking her for the coffee. Having finished with Cheryl, they both say goodbye to me, settle their bills with the receptionist, and exit the salon. Mr. T. still has not budged ! " Hey dude, you O.K. ? " i ask, " Don, who were those two girls ? they were gorgeous ! " " of course," I answer, " All my clients are gorgeous ! " " No, no ," he says, " They are exceptional ! what do they do ? " They manage a boutique in Fashion Valley " i inform him " Will you ask them if they will have dinner with us next week ? " " Mr. T, for you, i will make an exception and enquire if they are free for dinner " A week later, Saturday night, they have accepted the invitation, and chosen the night. Mr. T picks me up at my beach house, 7:30 P.M. he is dressed G.Q. designer jean jacket and jeans, no tie, except for gym work outs, this is the first time i've seen him without a tie. Mr. T was definitely wanting to appear " Cool ." On the way to the rendezvous, we decide that since neither of us has a preference, we will ultimately let the ladies make the choice. Arriving at the typical southern Californian bungalow, we leave the car and stroll to the front door, being first, i push the chime, immediately, the door opens, our progress had been observed !

But who is this ! i was unaware of a third room mate ! she is a Tisian painting, animated, bone china white skin, shoulder length flame red hair, Leopard green eyes, a 5' 4" body that glowed with kinetic

127

energy ! gathering my poise, i introduce Mr. T and myself, " Who else could you be ? " she says, and smiling, invites us in. Barbara and Cheryl are putting on their finishing touches, " Please be seated, may i offer you a glass of white Zinfedel ? " " Yes " i say, with enthusiasm. (the reply would have been the same had the offering been Hemlock !) Mr. T requests black coffee. Excusing herself, she departs for the kitchen. " Mr. T, what did she say her name was ? " He grinned and said " Pearl " it fitted. Having a few minutes to study the décor, i was surprised to see prints of Old masters and models,

depicting Haute couture of different, historic periods, all tastefully framed. NOTE : This was unusual for the 70s, it was De-rigeur to plaster posters of rock stars and Gurus on the walls, never framed !
the furniture was comfortable, nothing " over stuffed " or a bean bag in sight, subdued lighting, soft jazz on the stereo. Mr.T, not being a connoisseur of the arts, was sorting through the magazines on the coffee table, he says " I think we are in trouble, look what they are reading, Wall ST. Journal, Economic magazine and Forbes. Plus the top high fashion magazines, what was glaringly absent, was the ubiquitous

Hollywood gossip rags ! Mr. T was right, we were in trouble. Pearl, task accomplished, glides in from the kitchen, presents Mr. T with a chipped coffee mug that has " U.S. Navy " printed on it ! before i can say something clever, our dates make an entrance, Cheryl says, " Sorry to keep you waiting. " we both jump to our feet and say no problem, in unison, it was so un cool, everyone started laughing. From that moment on, we were destined to have a good night. (a pause is in order, the girls could have stepped off the cover of Cosmo ! Barbara is dressed in a little black raw silk dress that is so little, to quote Bob Hope ' You can't tell if she is outside trying to get in, or inside trying to get out ' black three inch Spikers, silver costume jewelry draped around a long slender neck. Cheryl, in contrast, is cocooned in a diaphanous, lemon, mid thigh, clinging Mandarin collar creation that reveals everything but shows nothing, matching tinted four inch heels and no other adornment, nothing is needed ! their

combined scent, perceived by the two horny males, pure animal musk ! a moment of small talk and we prepare to leave. Disaster strikes ! Mr. T, trying to be cool, drops his car keys, it was inevitable, considering his fumbling ineptitude at performing the simple task of removing them from his pocket. Making a sweeping movement in an attempt to charm the girls with his agility, Mr. T bends from the waist and in one fell swoop, retrieves the wayward keys, however, fate intercedes and decides his future for the next thirty years ! and still counting !. How can the simple act of picking up dropped keys dictate the future lives of two people ? you might ask. Simple, Mr.T's ungraceful act of picking up the keys, set in motion the order of choice of dinner partners. Barbara, having heard the distinct sound of a ripping seam, took Mr. T by the hand and said " I believe you have just ripped the seat of your pants." Seeing he was too embarrassed to speak, she said " Your coat is long enough to cover the problem, and if you won't tell anyone, i'm sure we can keep a secret. " This propelled us into a fit of laughter. Barbara became his dinner partner and they were married a year later, as for me and Cheryl, we became friends, but i was not to lose out, Pearl made an appointment two days later, and we had a great year together.

THE DEMISE OF A PARTY ANIMAL

Thursday : 6 P.M.
Client : Marsla
Marsla arrives with two friends, Chikita and Carmen, all three, friends and clients of five years, we have socialized much during this time. They are fiery hot blooded Latina's thick black hair, dancing brown eyes, olive radiant skin. Variations in height, all voluptuous and sexually active. If half the stories they told me were true ! NOTE : In the next decade, the Latin woman will be experienced in all her charms.
Marsla has been trimmed and as the blow dry is being finished, she asks me if i have any plans for the night " No " i say, " Is this the night i finally get lucky with all three of you ? " Chikita laughs and says "; No you dummy, you couldn't handle even one of us, you would die ! " i retort, " It would be a happy death ! " NOTE : Often hairdressers morph into an extended family with some clients, they were like sisters to me.
" Join us for drinks, " Carmen says, " Where ? " i ask. " Dos Amigos " she says. " The owners are clients of mine, it is the numero uno beach party club," " Give me ten minutes to check out, and i'll follow you." " Hurry " Marsla says, " Keep your pants on " i say, " What makes you think i have any on ? ! " she replies. The night is off to a good start.
Half an hour later we somehow arrive at Dos Amigos without being arrested, Latinas tend to drive like they live life, with gusto !

Having parked our cars we arrive at the front door, the doorman, smiling, opens the door for us, winks, and says " Enjoy " A hostess is waiting, she escorts us to a roped off area consisting of five fully occupied tables, Tom and Jerry have a table with four empty chairs, they are obviously for us. The party looks as though it has been going on for a while, empty Margaritas pitchers are being replaced with full ones by the staff. " Jerry, what is the occasion ? " i ask, Tom answers, " Just another day in paradise " The party does not look impromptu. The band stops, the room goes dark, a spotlight picks me out, and the band strikes up " Happy Birthday " everyone in the room joins in. From the kitchen, two topless bi kini clad girls, carrying a birthday cake with lots and lots of candles, (must have been about one hundred,) *the girls place the cake on the table. This is the only surprise birthday party of my life, what a party, all the girls danced with me and congratulated me with a big kiss and hug, even some who were not with our party happily joined in. what happened next is like the previous story of Mr. T. Trix, a girl at the next table bought a friend from her office , Trix was a recent U.C.L.A. graduate she brings her friend to the table, and introduces her, she is a 5' 6" Japanese girl, her name is Hollie, she shook hands with me ,Tom and Jerry, very formally and wished me a happy birthday. Twelve o'clock the party has wound down, the party goers are drifting into ever smaller groups of carnal interest, all determined to avoid a night un fulfilled. Tom takes an interest in Latina pulcutrude. Swaggering to our table, he asks what are the plans for the night, Chakita crosses her legs, forcing kinetic energy to pull her tightly clinging dress to within one inch of " Paradise " smiles and says " What did you have in mind ? " Tom takes a sip of a very large Tequila Sunrise and says " The three of you are invited to my house for a Jacuzzi party " Marsla, Chakita and Carmen huddle for a moment, reaching a unanimous decision, Chikita says " Lets party ! " Tom turns to me, " Have you seen Jerry ? " " No, not since he was introduced to Hollie "*

Tom says "; Maybe he will show up later, lets go." " Tom, i love all three of these girls but we don't have sex, they are all good friends, besides, I have someone waiting for me, you have a good time and thanks for coming to the birthday party." Three days later, he calls me at work, " Don, the girls almost killed me ! however, the reason i called, we have lost Jerry ! " My heart stopped for a second ! visions of Jerry wiping out in his Testarrossa flashed through my mind, fearing the worst, i ask " What happened ? " " Remember the girl he met at your party, the gorgeous Japanese ? " Tom says, " Yes, i remember her, what's happened ? "Jerry is in Hawaii, he called me to tell me they got married ! , now what do you think of that ! "   " You're pulling my leg right ? " " No, all too true, we have lost a party animal. " Jerry never came to another Jacuzzi party, they have been married twenty eight years, and have two beautiful children.

FOREVER YOUNG

Client ; Dr. Bob

He is a prominent oral surgeon, he is a sixty something, very trim, addicted cyclist, he never misses the yearly Baja race T. J. to

Hussan's Cantina (everyone who rides a bike should do this at least once in their lives.) He was hesitant the first time he came in for a styling, men of that generation, when they were young, would never have set foot in a beauty salon ! his daughter, a client of five years gave him a gift voucher. Dr. Bob has been a client now for four months. Learning that i had served in the air force, he shared stories with me about English ladies he had danced with NOTE : This, for him, meant sexual relationship. when he flew B17s in World war Two.

Thursday 1 P.M. Client : Betty
A real estate agent and attractive divorced, forty something, is getting her highlights touched up, Bob, my next appointment, has come in half an hour early, my assistant places him in the chair next to me and Betty, we say hello and i introduce him to Betty. She is entertaining us with office jokes, they tend to be risqué. Dr Bob is straining to hear the punch lines, he chuckles, he is finding her candour amusing, fifteen minutes flies by. A pause in Betty's running commentary prompts Dr. Bob to phrase an un timely question. " Don, how much longer before you are ready for me ? " Betty turns her head, looks at Dr. Bob, as if to say " who is this creature ? " and in a devil may care, tone, with one eyebrow arched, says " What better do you have to do ? " " No, no ! " Dr. Bob exclaims, " I was hoping you would be staying longer. " Betty pauses and with a patent " you will love this house " smile, says " What would you like to do ? " Bob gathers himself, " Maybe we could go for a coffee when Don finishes " " I'm coffee'd out " she says " I have a better idea, lets go across the road to The Gulls, have a glass of wine, and watch the sun go down." Betty waited until Dr. Bob was cut and blow dried, they departed for The Gulls. It was a glorious sunset.

Wednesday 2:30 P.M.
Client: Cassandra.
She is Dr. Bob's daughter, two weeks have elapsed since his introduction to Betty, Cassandra is a first year med. student, she seems happy today, i received a big hug when my assistant bought her, freshly shampooed, to my chair, " Don," she says, " I can't believe my father, he is acting like a teenager in heat ! he and betty have been in separable ! " " All this enlightenment, before we decide on your cut, it must be serious ! " i say. She laughs, we decide on a long layered cut, framing her face. " Don, since mum

died, ten years ago, this is the first relationship he has had, mum and dad met in grade school, i don't think they ever dated anyone else, he asked me yesterday how i felt about him dating." " What did you tell him ? "
" Go for it ! " good advice.

Tuesday 4:00 P.M.
Client DR. Bob
It is now two months since he and Betty enjoyed their first sunset and glass of wine together. They have come in together for their appointments, his daughter was right, everyone smiles at their romantic behavior it is contagious, like yawning. Dr. Bob is in my chair, " Don, i don't know how to thank you." He says, " I never believed for one moment that love would enter my life again, after my wife left this world, only Cassandra kept my life from being an empty void, friends introduced nice ladies to me, but there was no spark, Betty is different, on our first date, dinner at Mr. A's. NOTE : Mr. A's is a famous San Diego, high rise, restaurant, you are level with landing aircraft ! Good wine, two short hours of conversation, i have no idea what we talked about, she reached across the table, took my hand, and i swear she said take me home and fuck my brains out ! Don, my wife never said that to me " " Women have come a long way. " i told him. Ten years of marital bliss later, they visited me on their second honeymoon in Costa Rica.

A TRUCK DRIVING MAN
AND THE PROFESSOR

Saturday, 1 P.M.
Client : Beatrice
A widowed mother of one, Beatrice is a fifty something years young surgical nurse, a valued client of five years, she has medium light brown hair with a light frosting of grey, with her trim figure and youthful attitude, she easily passes for a thirty something.

Today she is making a big leap, and finally taking my advice to have her hair tinted. i can see she seems preoccupied, " Don't worry, you will look great." "Sorry Don, it's not my hair, i have often talked about my son, as you know, he is constantly in trouble with his employers, he has been fired for the second time this year, he has now informed me that he is going to enroll in a school that teaches big rig truck driving, James was eight when his father was killed in Vietnam, he is a troubled kid, and it worries me that maybe it's my fault. " " Beatrice, you have been a good mother, it's just the times we are in." NOTE : During the Vietnam war, and long after it was over, the salon had many clients who were trying to raise children alone."

" Don, if i can persuade him to have a different haircut, will you do it ? " Of course, i style lots of young guys hair, send him in," " If you can persuade him to dress more conservatively for the interview, it might help " " But Beatrice, what are you not telling me ? " she smiles sadly, and after a moment, says " James has curly hair like his father, it is very long and bushy." " A challenge is good ! i will look forward to meeting him. "

Saturday 1:00 P.M.

Client : James
I see why his mother is concerned, James is 6' 3" 220 Lbs. he is dressed like Marlon Brando's character in " The Wild One " jeans, biker boots, black leather motorcycle jacket, T shirt, he is trying to act cool. My assistant is used to " first time " male clients, she approaches James with a big smile and says " We are ready for you, please follow me. " (He meekly obeys, it does not hurt that my assistant is drop dead gorgeous, we men are all the same, a pretty face, warm smile, and we have no defense !) Shampoo finished, she escorts James to my chair, i extend my hand, he shakes it with considerable force, matching him with equal force, he looks surprised, the pecking order has been established. " Hop in the chair " i say " Let's see what we can do for you " " Mum told me you could do something with my hair, i'm here to keep her happy " " No James " i say, You are

here because you are worried about your interview and you don't want to disappoint your mother. " He is quiet for a second, looks in the mirror and says " You're right." " Don't worry, we will make a new you, one even a mother could love. " He laughs, the ice is broken.

It was a challenge, i layered his hair, and shortened it by 4" This exposed his facial bone structure. Letting his hair dry naturally we are both surprised by the result, it is a metamorphosis. My assistant tells James, " You look like Jon Bon Jovi " his smile as he looks in the mirror is ample reward for those in my profession.

A month has passed.

Thursday 1:00 P.M.

Client : Beatrice

She is in for her touch up. " Don, James was accepted in the driving school, your hair cut and the new suit did it. "

This is the story of his achievements : -

Five years have sped by, James now owns three eighteen wheelers. He is waiting having come in early, the assistants are buzzing round him like bees to a honey pot ! he looks like a "G.Q." centerfold Armani sport coat, designer jeans, silk shirt, Gucci loafers (Only in America !)

Friday 4:30 P.M.

Client :

Sharon.

Sharon is a professor in mathematics in a junior college, she is 26, a native Californian, 5' 10" tanned, with big, green eyes, and being Californian, a natural blonde. Her sport, competitive Beach Volleyball We have been talking about her match this weekend. " Don, this is a semi final, if we win, the state final is in Santa Monica, why don't you bring your girlfriend along on Sunday, it's by "Hamills" (a famous surf shop) on P.B." " Sharon, i would love to see you win, but I have plans for a San Francisco weekend, i promise i will be there for the Championship play off. " she laughs and says " Good enough. " The trim and blow dry finished, she says goodbye and that she hopes I have a good time in San Francisco. All the stylists line up and give her a " Hi Five" as she leaves.

Friday 5:00 P.M. (same day)

Client :

James.

He was shampooed and waiting in my second chair, i gesture to him and say for him to come over to the ocean view chair, he doesn't answer but comes and sits down, " How have you been ? " i ask, still no answer, he looks at me like a third grader who has just lost his candy to the school bully. " Who was that girl ? " he stammers. As i never give information about clients, i suggest he goes to the Beach Volleyball match.

One month later, Saturday 1:30 P.M.
Client : Sharon.
As she arrives, the stylists congratulate her on the win. While cutting her hair, she tells me about the match. " Don, i have a question for you, remember the guy who was waiting for you last time i was here? " "Yes, his name is James, why ? " " He was at the match, and when we won, he gave a rose to me and Janis, we were surrounded with friends and i never got the chance to thank him, could you do it for me next time you see him ? " " I have a better idea, Sharon, leave me your card, that way you can thank him. " she smiles, reaches into her purse, and with mathematical precision, produces her card and presents it to me. " I'll be waiting." She says as she leaves.

Two weeks later.
Tuesday 10:00 A.M.
Client: James.
He is my first client of the day, and the first of the week. My assistant, having finished the shampooing, has deposited him in my chair. As she enters the back room, where i have been listening to the weekend exploits of my fellow stylists, mostly excursions into the absurd, Patty, my assistant tells me James is waiting and he seems "on edge" That's very odd, apart from his first time here, he is normally totally relaxed. i thank Patty and leave our "Den of inequity" and head for my agitated client, as i approach, he is nervously tapping his fingers on the chair. "Good morning James, how's life ? " " Good." he replies. Then with a sheepish smile, adds " Well, maybe, depends on how you can help me." "Sure, what do you need ? " " I went to the Beach Volleyball match as you suggested, Sharon and her partner won, there is a flower stall next to Hamills, so i bought two roses, no problem giving one to each of them but there was a mob surrounding them and I had no chance to talk." " So what do you want from me ? " I ask, trying not to smile " What does Sharon do ? " finishing a short "Bio" of her, James is crestfallen he looks like someone who was backing out of their drive, and ran over their puppy ! he takes a second, then says " Don, you have known me since i was a jerk. "

" No James, you were never a jerk, just a guy that needed direction . " " Thanks, but she would never be interested in a truck driver. " " Why don't you let her decide." I open the drawer, take out her

card and hand it to him. " She told me to give you this. " his face lit up like he had just discovered the meaning of life ! . . . . . .
As they say in the movies . . . to be continued . . . .

THE GOOD THE BAD AND THE UGLY

The Sunshine Factory was a microcosm of the outside world, and as such, it produced hairdressers who would be a credit to the profession.

THE GOOD : -

Jean Brae started her highly successful career at The Sunshine Factory, she went on to become Paul Mitchell stage partner, and contributed greatly to his domination of the market.

THE BAD : -

A stylist who began his career with The Sunshine Factory, showed much promise, however, not wishing to invest the amount of time all professions demand, he decided, along with an accomplice, to rob "Yum Yum" (Donut Franchise) this was his "Night Job"
They terrorized the Yum Yum world of San Diego for several months before they made the mistake of a daytime robbery, two of San Diego's finest happened to be on a "donut run" and thus, ended the infamous "Yum Yum Banditos" reign of incompetence.

THE UGLY
The saga of a part time female receptionist.
She and her boyfriend became the modern day equivalent of "Bonnie & Clyde" They proceeded to rob several businesses in San Diego County, tiring of the hard work, the geniuses had an epiphany, why not rob someone who drove an expensive car and looked rich, prowling a shopping center parking lot late at night, they found a well dressed gentleman driving a Cadillac, when he parked and exited the vehicle, they pounced, relieving him of his credit cards, cash and Rolex, they then rendered him unconscious and deposited him in the trunk of the car. Here is where it gets strange, the Cadillac, being a better ride than their pickup they decided to use it for several days. A neighbors dog became curious about the smell emanating from the vehicle and naturally, displaying great interest in it drew the attention of his master, which led to a 911 call being made leading to the subsequent arrest of the villains who are now residing as guests of the Californian custodial system.

SUMMATION OF THE 70's

The great party

The 70's.from the beginning, were to be different from the past decade (Tune in, Turn on & Drop out) was a mantra now no longer in vogue, a new chant swept the land (Conspicuous Consumerism) America was in need of a respite. Disco nights was the new Opium for the masses, Disco Dans and dancing queens performed with abandon on the dance floors of a nation. Women who became of age in the 70's no longer accepted communal sex as a higher plane of awareness, they saw it as a subornation of their bodies. L.S.D. was no longer the "Trip" most sought after, Pot, by it's application, had ruled itself defunct, you could not smoke a joint in disco restrooms, however, you could "Razor" a line of Coke and if you were really "Hip" you snorted it through a rolled up 100 Dollar bill, or, as some more hedonistic women preferred, they applied it in generous amounts to their clitoris. Sex and wealth had reached a convergence. Champagne flowed like The Nile and Ferraris roared out a primeval scream of pure lust.

In the salon, clients, both male and female, are sharing with me the fulfillment and satisfactions of their relationships and do not preclude the invitation to others to share their desires and fantasies. When sexologists and sexual behaviorists study the decade of the 70's I believe they will find this short 10 years is the happiest period of sexual awareness our species has ever known.

FASHION WOMEN

The fashion houses of Europe, having been rendered impotent in the sixties, were determined to wrest back control of what they presumed was their divine right to dictate the length of women's dresses.

The masses rose up and stormed the barricades of Haute Couture. Once having seen the inside of a ladies thigh in polite society, never more would the display of an ankle or panty hosed knee be sufficient ! Johnny Carson " The Late Show " when Johnny's guests appeared in the "Midi " the ladies were T.V. and film's most sexy actresses, they were met with moans from the audience by both men and women. At the halfway point, they excused themselves, saying they had other commitments, they went to the dressing room, and changed into the " Mini " and returned to a standing ovation, by both the men and women of the audience, needless to say, the "Midi" had died. The upside, small younger minded fashion houses grew into the giants of today, NOTE : today at high school dances, the " Fashion Police" have been checking under girl's dresses for the forbidden thong ! You can never put the Genie back in the bottle !

FASHION MEN

Once again, an English invasion, this time the liberation of men's fashion from Hollywood to the Board room designer suits made from re cycled blue jeans (mainly Levis) coats and pants were constructed of patches in various states of used Denim. Bell bottom pants, no longer exclusively Navy uniform apparel, the well turned out young, are not so young C.E.O's from blow dried, layered hair to ankle high English boots, silk shirts, gold chain necklace, sometimes several ! remember Mr. T of "The A Team" gold bracelet and rings. The 70's male was ready to face the jungle. In the mid 70's double knit leisure suits Nik Nik shirts replaced natural fibre in men's apparel. NOTE : Now the fad in fashion is to "Go Green " whatever that means !

HAIR WOMEN

My industry had the same challenge to meet as the clothing industry. Those who listened to the young, prospered. An interview in Vogue, the great Paris designer "Che Vonche" when asked where he drew his inspiration from, replied, " Very simple, I visit a coffee house in Mont Maitre, sit at an outside table, and observe the La Salvge as they promenade, the energy of youth is reflected in their fashion statements." It was the same for my industry, the "Lion's Mane " brought young women back to the salon, Sun streaking, first observed in surfers, when modified for the salon, made them Californian girls, wherever they lived !

HAIR MEN

The revolution in men's hairstyling equaled that of women, Barbers did not learn the new methods introduced by Vidal Sassoon and Paul Mitchel. The impact of "Shampoo" the movie, made it de rigeur to patronize the salons.

PROLOGUE
YUPPIEISM / THE 80s

The end of a decade is a small death it is an ending with a soul weariness felt through all layers of society, but out of the ashes of the old, new dreams arise. The air vibrates in anticipation of new wonders to come. The fashion industry is no exception, no one can predict the new trends. Bell bottom pants, platform shoes for men, receded into the graveyard of banality. Hairdressers 'star image' enjoyed in the 70s would morph into a new vibrant professionalism, we became business orientated.

Professional product companies endeavored to place their goods on beauty salon shelves, most failed, they lacked the 'magic' the fashion world demands.

The amalgamation of a hairdresser and a dreamer, a combination that changed the constraints of the beauty industry.

QUOTE : With the princely sum of 700 Dollars, John Paul De Joria and the late Paul Mitchell had a vision, to found a company by hairdressers, for hairdressers. So simple a business plan, it's ultimate success lay in it's uniqueness.

My association with Paul Mitchell systems, was in the future.

TEN, THE MOVIE

Ten exploded on the silver screen like a comet, it's presence felt around the world. Hollywood, with this, at best, (B) picture, set the standard by which women's beauty became measured, '10' being the ultimate. Bo Derek, an hitherto unknown became the symbol of perfection. Like the 'Farrah' of the 70s, it was the hairstyle that made the woman famous, the style caught hairdressers totally un prepared, the beauty school system was not integrated, I had no idea how to create a '10', the Sunshine Factory 'got lucky' i was dating an Afro-American model, she saw the problem the salon was having and introduced me to a friend of hers who just happened to be an Afro American hairdresser, after much pleading with Marge to come to the salon and teach the staff how to create the style, she eventually agreed NOTE : A considerable amount of 'Uncle Bens' helped.

Without the help of Marge, and the two assistants she brought with her, what follows could not have been possible.

SAN DIEGO REGISTER
Sunday, January 20th 1980
By Alison Darosa

QUOTE :
" The movie '10' is yanking the hairstyling industry out of the doldrums, actress Bo Derek's hairstyle in the movie, i.e. shoulder length braids adorned with beads and feathers, is the biggest fashion trend since ice skater, Dorothy Hamil introduced her sassy version of the precision cut to American women. " say salon operators, "When the movie '10' made it's big splash, we started getting calls straight away from people who wanted us to transform them from 8's to 10's " said Don Davis, co owner of The Sunshine Factory " You're an automatic '10' if you adopt that style, women who consider themselves 8's are more than ready to become 10's but it's men, especially in their late thirties, forties and fifties (according to Don Davis) who are the root of 10's success, perhaps these men identify with the star, Dudley Moore, who, in his mid life crisis found his '10' at any rate, it's the middle aged, more sophisticated man who is most eager lady to become a '10' by having that hairstyle."

SALON IMPACT

They literally came by the bus load ! 'The Legal Wives Club', as the name suggests, were the spouses of lawyers, they resided in a community 40 miles north of San Diego, having seen the article in 'The Register', and being adventurous (not un common in lawyers wives.) The club booked the salon, exclusively on a Monday, the lady who made the booking, assured me there would be 20 eager 'wanna be', '10s'
08: 00 A. M. Monday, a chartered bus arrives, 20 ladies ranging in ages from 20s to mid 40s, descend on The Sunshine Factory, they did not travel light, 2, 'Star foam' chests containing bottles of iced Champagne, accompanied the entourage. Every time a '10' was 'born' one and all drank a toast. It was an exhilarating day. The following week, we received 'thank you notes from grateful husbands, all wrote " It was a night to remember ! "

Wednesday 02 : 00 P. M.
Client: Mrs. Smith
Mrs. Smith was 62 years young, the most senior lady i had the pleasure of enhancing with a '10' this is the story of how her appointment came about. On a very busy Friday, the receptionist approaches me and says " Don, there is a gentleman on the phone who insists on speaking with you." " Are you sure you can't handle it ? " i ask. " I think you should speak to him, he is requesting a special service. " my client, overhearing the conversation, says " I'm enjoying watching the surfers, go ahead and take the call. "

Picking up the phone, i ask how may i help. A very strong assertive voice asks " Is this Mr. Davis ? " " Yes" i reply inquisitively " Good, i should like to make an appointment next Saturday for my wife, she will require a '10' " pausing for a moment, i tell him Saturday is a busy day and producing a '10' can take almost the entire day, could she make it in on Thursday ? he replies. " Mr. Davis, how much do you usually make on a Saturday ? " a strange question, but for some reason i answer that i average around 500 Dollars. " There will be a check delivered to the salon, let me know if it is not sufficient. " and with that, he hangs up the phone. Two hours later, a gentleman in a black suit is waiting at the front desk. Marge gestures for me to come over, i approach the desk and ask what the problem is. " You are Mr. Davis ? " the black suit enquires. " Yes, that's me. " He takes an elegant envelope from his briefcase and hands it to me saying " Have a good day." Turns, and walks out. " Marge, who was that ? " " I don't know " she replies. " Why don't you open the envelope ? " she suggests. i hand it back to her saying " You do the honors, i've got a client waiting." Five minutes later, Marge is at my station, " What did it say ? " i ask " You'd better look at it. " she says and hands me a check written out to the sum of 1,000 Dollars, but it was the name on it that was the biggest shock, Mr. Smith was one of California's most renowned land developers.
Saturday, 09 : 00 A. M.
Client : Mrs. Smith
She is an attractive lady, and has a remarkable resemblance to Katherine Hepburn she is charming, and a good trouper, during the

next six hours, she entertains me and my assistant with anecdotes about some of Hollywood's stars from the 'Golden Era' " I am curious, why did you decide to have a '10' ? I ask, she explains,

" My husband and i attended a private screening of "TEN" and were both reminded of our honeymoon in Acapulco, i told him it would have been so sexy to have had that hairstyle, Sunday is our 40th anniversary and we are flying to Acapulco to celebrate, my husband insisted i have that style for the occasion. " Do you think it's appropriate for someone of my age ? " I told her Bo Derek had nothing on her !

(TEN) WHY

I believe neither 'Ten', the movie, nor Bo Derek would have made the impact, which is still felt to this day, without the hairstyle, why does it cause such arousal of the male libido ? did the women of ancient Egypt know something, thousands of years ago ? women are depicted in the paintings in Egyptian tombs wearing 10s it is the only style that evokes feelings of raw carnality in the male, as i sit in the Vivaldi coffee shop Costa Rica, young girls drift by, 'Mall cruising' i notice that the ones with 10s get the most attention from young male admirers, and one old one too !

BIMMER'S

In the eighties, women are aggressively asserting their presence in corporate America, the business world will be greatly enhanced by their arrival, my male clients, not being prepared for this invasion, are telling me of their anxieties.

Client : Ralafee

He is a Middle Easterner who is a graduate of Wharton, his major, International finance.

Thursday : 4:30 P.M.

Rolafee has been shampooed and is in my chair, he and his wife have been clients of three years. NOTE : Usually, male clients talk about fast cars and women before they talk about themselves.

Ten minutes into the cut, " Don, i have a problem, has my wife spoken to you about her offer from a major New York investment firm ? " " Yes, she has mentioned it. " " I don't know what to do, we are disagreeing as to whether she should accept or not, her pay package and stock options make me feel inferior, i love Dorothy, but my Middle Eastern up bringing is in conflict with the situation." " Think about it this way, we are only men, we ARE inferior. " my assistant agreed, we both laugh. Dorothy accepted the offer, i lost two clients.

Wednesday 3:30 P.M.
Client : June
She heads her own real estate office.
June is having a tint touch up, " Don, how's your love life." this
usually implies i should return the question, ('Women can be very
direct ') i oblige. She smiles, " My ex-husband wants us to get back
together, the big problem is that my girl friends and i, as you are
aware, take vacations around the world with Club Med, we meet
interesting men, i don't want to give that up, it makes me feel young
again." You are young ! " i tell her. " Thanks, i love you." " Hey,
that was your third marriage, do whatever makes you happy."
They didn't get back together, i was invited to her fourth wedding, a
doctor she met at 'Club Med', he was five years younger than her.

Thursday 05:00 P.M.
Client: Willard.

He is a thirty something, U.C.L.A. graduate in ocean research.
I have finished cutting his hair, and letting it dry naturally, he is my
last client of the day and we are watching the 'Beachnicks' perform
their mating rituals. "Don, may i ask you a question ? " (this really
means he wants to tell me something.) " You know my girlfriend, Allen
cuts her hair, do you ever talk to her ? " " Only to say hello, why ?
" " O.K here goes, Rhonda and i have been dating for two years,
last week, she gave me an ultimatum, she said it was time to plan for
our future, she presented me with a list of stock investments we
should consider, if we plan wisely, we can retire in twenty five years,
and travel, our two children will be in college." What children ? "

i ask " The two we set up the college fund for. " " Don, this seems
so planned." " Do you love her ? " " Yes, very much." He says "
You just answered you own question, have a good life. "
25 years later, they visited Costa Rica , still very much in love. (the two
children doing very well in college)

V.C.R.   DATING

V.C.R. analogue, was all the rage in the 80s, entrepreneurs are opening dating clubs. For a fee, a sociologist interviews you on tape, to determine the relationship you are seeking, club members, based on their interviews, are sent tapes of prospective mates.

Tuesday, 10:00 A.M.
Client : Peggy
She has a Liberal Arts degree U.C.S.D. Peggy is my first appointment, shoulder length light brown hair, today is a first for her, the big step, 'Surfer Girl' sun streaks, usually clients are apprehensive when making a dramatic change, but Peggy always seemed so in control, today is different, her concentration is not on the procedure. " Is something bothering you ? " i ask, " Yes, i have contemplated changing the color of my hair, it always seemed so superficial, people should consider what's in my head, not on it." " Why did you change your mind ? " she lets out a big sigh, this means the truth is coming. " Don, you won't believe what i've done, three weeks ago, not being happy with my social life, i joined a V.C.R. dating club. My interviewer suggested that i should change my image to meet the kind of men that would find me attractive, they introduced me to a personal shopper   NOTE : Personal shoppers were all the rage of the 80s. she changed my wardrobe completely, so, now you know, what do you think ? "   " It's always fun to enhance your image, the interviewer was right, our persona is how people react to us. Hollywood is the master of perception, what you see is what you get." " But Don, isn't that being phony ? "   " Yes and no, you are who you think you are, since we have to wear clothes, style our hair, why not enjoy the experience. " Peggy dated several different men she met through the video dating club, one year later, she married a doctor she met while shopping in ' Ralphs.' they were both squeezing fruit.

153

THINGS TO REMEMBER

" Ten " was interesting from a racial perspective, this was 15 years before 'Rap' it was the first hair fashion to cross racial lines.

For better or worse, men and women rate each other, based on a hypothetical equation $0 + 5 + 5 = 10$ i.e perfection.

The first response was negative from afro American hairdressers, after the article appeared in the newspaper, however, after persuading a few to give Sunshine Factory stylists lessons, all was well.

FLASH DANCE

The influence Hollywood has on our lives is strange, "Flash Dance" did not launch a new hairstyle, leg warmers and 'off the shoulder' sweatshirts, once seen only in gymnasiums, became the latest fashion craze. Jennifer Beales, the star of Flash Dance, did launch the search for ethnic actresses (J. Lo / Penelope Cruz / Holly Berry.) owe a debt of gratitude to Jennifer Beales. For those of you that were too young, to have seen it, she portrays a modern day Cinderella.

"Urban Cowboy" the movie, John Travolta. Fashion wise 'Tonny Lama Boots' became part of the lexicon, president Ronald Reagan had a custom made pair featuring the American flag, Jordache sold tons of boot flare jeans but of the two movies, there was no defining hair statement. The world of hair fashion, like nature, abhors a vacuum, as usual it would be youth that sets the trend, this time, all of society would be shocked, the era of Punk had arrived !

In the mid 80s surfers were being seen with military short, hair cuts with long spikey tops and the colors were expressions of every combination of the rainbow. Bart Simpson would later copy the Punks.

THE GREAT CRISIS

PUNK MANIA

As I write this tome, America is in the grip of the greatest financial disconnect in a century. Beginning in the early 80s my industry was faced with it's greatest challenge, out of west Hollywood and the benign beaches of the Golden State, came forth the 'Punks' vibrating with what some of the establishment considered an obscene art form, I loved them ! however, hairdressers had no clue as to how to duplicate this fresh new fashion statement. There were no electric clippers in beauty salons , there was no requirement by the state cosmetologist board for clipper technique. Basically, we panicked. Paul Mitchell systems to the rescue, Jean Brae, Paul's stage partner, visited the Sunshine Factory often, to teach us new Paul Mitchell product knowledge. The breakthrough, Jean told us Paul was in Scotland to observe a tool that could simplify clipper use. Brian Drum, the inventor of the 'Flat Topper' , saved us.

Lori suggested we invite Punks to participate as models. We sought out the most outrageous examples. When you participate with your model, in executing a design, the learning curve accelerates by 50% after a month of experimenting on models, the Sunshine Factory was ready.

PUNK AS A LIFESTYLE

Client: Sundance, Tuesday 2:30 P.M.

Sundance is my baptismal to the world of Punk, all heads turn as she enters the salon. Approaching the appointment desk, she is totally self assured, like a Prima Donna Ballerina, her every gesture is being evaluated, most with envy, it would require the brush of Pablo Picasso to do justice to this animated canvas, a kaleidoscope of clashing colors, a whirlpool of circles and lines none of the angles of which seemed to balance, yet there was a rhythm of conflux held together with an air of distain. Sundance was recommended to me by a U.C.S.D. client. Sundance was a third year music major, I smiled as she approached my station, in a very quiet voice, she said, "I am Sundance." " Who else could you possibly be. " I said. We both laugh. Shoran, my assistant, gently guides Sundance to a shampoo bowl. Five minutes later shampooing and conditioning performed, she is in my chair. " Don, I need to tone down just a little bit, what do you suggest ? " " Why do you need to tone down ? " " Mom and dad are visiting this weekend. " " O.K. understood. Using the 'Flat Topper', the sides are shortened, this was my first use of the clippers on a paying client, the top was cut and spiked with shears, it looked great, most important , it was fun. Within six months, the salon would be doing softer and more subtle versions of Punk on all ages of men and women. Sundance calls me the next day and invites me to a Punk 'Happening", i accept.

PARTY PUNKERS

Sundance lived in a cottage in Hillcrest, an art enclave. I left my car in her driveway. The party was five blocks, a ten minute stroll on an enchanted San Diego night., this gave me ample time to enjoy her costume, the dress was in multiple long strips of gauze, fastened at the waist with a band of brightly hued feathers, held together in some mysterious way. Around a delicate, slender neck, was a bronze hoop with flowing strips of tie dyed linen, descending to her waist in front and to her hips at the back. White leather, woven sandals with Hindu prayer bells on thin golden chains circling each ankle which chimed as she walked. Hair, a spiked, blue and white statement. All 5' 8" was a living animated ' Dali – esque ' creation. The streets were populated with 'La Savage' of all sexes, some, impossible to distinguish between. Sundance drew hungry eyes from all we passed , she was a zephyr blowing through the streets of Sodom and Gomorrah.

THE HAPPENING

The party was in a warehouse dating from the 1920's gothic chandeliers with designer electric candles. The music, Pink Floyd and the sex pistols (the only two I recognized) for the first time I sensed a new generation was passing me by. In the wee hours of the morning, Sundance tells me it's time to go. I am her obedient servant. My mind has been fired with the unlimited color and designs of sheer, hair artistry. This was a new approach, much needed in the fashion industry. We are hand in hand as we enter the cottage, the walk has restored my energy, gently she pulls me towards her, no words are needed. Sweet lips, a warm tongue, we disengage, Sundance floats around, the room is lit by five giant candles, in wrought iron holders. Beethoven is placed on the turntable, the artist, Van Gellis, on the Moog synthesizer. Sundance removes her creation with grace and beauty, that only a woman in passion as old as Eve can offer a man. A body as white as pure Marble, un blemished by pubic hair, a tattooed serpent, coiled around one thigh, as she walked towards me in the flickering light, the image of the serpent disappeared into her mucus moist mouth of life.

It is said that the best compliment a man can make to a woman, is to remember her, Sundance is defiantly remembered !

I HAVE AN EPIPITHENY

Having mastered to some degree, the use of the electric clippers, in discussions with my fellow stylists we compared notes on the limitations of clipper cutting, we could not use our fingers as guides as we did with scissors, this greatly reduced our creativity. One day, between clients, watching surfers catching the curl, a thought germinated in my mind, what if a comb was curved ? might it be possible to cut along the curved surface, and by so doing, create curves in hair designs. No manufacturers of curved combs were to be found, after much trial and error, I arrived at a process of bending large, straight combs into different degrees of curvature. These prototypes were given to Sunshine factory stylists, in one week, an electric undercurrent seemed to flow through the salon. We were cutting designs never before imagined. This was a revolution in the art of hair cutting. On advice from a client who was an attorney, I filed for and was granted a U.S. patent for the curved comb, not only that but I was granted a patent for the cutting technique. This is the only patent granted for any form of hair cutting technique. It was time to offer the geodesic format to the cosmetologist profession. In past chapters I told of a girl who started at the Sunshine Factory and then, through hard work, became Paul Mitchell's stage partner and was instrumental in launching Paul Mitchell Systems. I called Jean and invited her for a demonstration, she was impressed with the 'Curve' and immediately saw the possibilities.

THE MASTER ARRIVES

I finally get to meet Paul Mitchell, two weeks after the demonstration, Jean brought Paul to the Sunshine Factory, he immediately understood the concept, to my surprise, after observing the cutting technique, he insisted on cutting a model. Ten minutes into the cut, he was pursuing innovations i had not thought of, i should have known, after all he was Paul Mitchell !

We broke for lunch, Jean, Paul and me, walked to (
Paul was astounded by the Sunshine Factory's locatic
salon had the most extraordinary view of any he ha
Over lunch, he asked for an exclusive agreement to market the
'Curve' under the Paul Mitchell Logo.
The next year was a learning experience New York Jacob Javit's
Center, the biggest trade show in our industry, 30 - 40 thousand
hairdressers in four days, venture through the booths and showrooms
exhibiting every conceivable product used in our profession. The Paul
Mitchell booth is the biggest and most popular in the event. Two
stages, thirty feet apart connected by the sales area. On each
stage, two chairs manned by Paul Mitchell associates who alternate
every hour, the Paul Mitchell associates have come from both big
cities, and small towns across America, this is the Mecca for
hairdressers.
The moment of truth, the Paul Mitchell booth was located 40' within
the main entrance, hairdressers were so amazed with the exhibition
that the sheer density made it impossible to enter the trade show,
The Jacob Javits staff all earned their pay for the next four days.
The Paul Mitchell associates never stopped, the 'Curve' succeeded way
beyond my expectations.

PAUL MITCHELL ASSOCIATES PARTY ON

The third day is a traditional party, Paul Mitchell associates
rendezvous at Astis, in the village, the staff sing aires from the best
Italian composers with gusto, after several toasts, the Paul Mitchell
people join in. the room was packed to capacity. Stylists representing
other lines, joined in with the camaraderie. A famous New York
hairdresser invites us to his 'Loft'. Being unable to make sense of the
bill, J.P. co-owner of Paul Mitchell, was having dinner with
distributors in a quieter, less rawkus room, settles the problem in an
act of magnificent altruism, he picks up the check. Paul Mitchell
master associates. Tom, having been to the Loft before, like the
Pied Piper, leads the way. We pour out of Astis, traffic stops,
pedestrians stare, even a Police cruiser slows, New York's finest, eye
us with suspicion. If you have ever been to New York you will be
aware that it is almost impossible to attract the jaded curiosity of a
native New Yorker.
Fifty more or less, performing artist, top of the hairdressers feeding
chain, in costumes as varied as the products they represent, is an
oddity even for The Big Apple.

160
/ 24

161
/ 25

162
/ 26

NEW YORK NIGHTS
LOFTING

The Loft, only a short walk away, gave us much needed time to clear our senses. It is magnificent, in a previous life, a manufacturer of steel wire. The mavens of New York go un challenged for there insight to change the unsightly to the most sought after. Best example, Donald Trump, developer extraordinaire.

163 / 27

The floor's century old, scarred Oak, now sanded and bleached white. The walls, a mixture of stone, brick and white plaster. Thirty five feet above the main floor, half of the second floor had been removed, which gave a vast open area. The ceiling, at least fifty feet from where i stood, the roof, a glassed skylight. I subsequently learnt, the lighting effect was the work of a famous Broadway stage designer. As i said earlier, the host was a famous New York salon owner and stylist. The night was a coupling of kindred spirits.

All artists, regardless of the art form, live outside the norms found in contemporary society. The difference in our medium, we touch the living results of our creations, entwining us into their lives.

Several intimate contacts, made at the party, were reported over the next three years at major trade shows across the United States. Like most hairdressers, i have frequented many trade shows, all hairdressers must attend the New York show. The scale of knowledge is beyond comprehension. You will return to your salon inspired, this i promise you.

164 / 28

CALIFORNIA DREAMS END

Doing multiple trade shows as well as Paul Mitchell distributor events, where i reside, is no longer important, on the recommendation of a client in 1984, i visited a country little known at that time, fact being, that when i asked my travel agent to book a flight, she thought it was an island, only one flight a week from L.A.X. on their national airline. The country; Costa Rica. The agent could only find a listing for two hotels, San Jose, The Corrobici, and the Jaco Beach Hotel.

The population of Costa Rica, at the time, was one and a half million, there are now an estimated three million weary souls. Following my visits between 1984 and 88, relocation there seemed like a good idea.

REMEMBERANCE

The final week leading up to the end of the Sunshine Factory sojourn, is fond memories and hundreds of clients stopped by to watch the last sunset, some, children when their parents brought them, are now parents themselves. It was a happy time, the popping of corks was heard all week, the Champagne flowed.

Two clients from the beginning years, Nikki was nine when her mother brought her in. she patiently sat and waited until I finished with her mother, while her mother was settling the bill, Nikki approached me and asked if i would do her hair next time, i told her it would be my privilege to cut her hair. During the ensuing years, she became like the daughter i never had.

The final day, she hired a professional performer, who entered the salon, disguised as a bag lady, she sat a 'Boom Box' on the floor and played the 'Stripper' music while dancing and stripping down to a 'G' string, and tassels, somehow fastened to her nipples ! the salon went wild ! it was a great surprise, and i still have the photo's to prove it. Other stylists were in hysterics, at last, someone had got even with me for all the practical jokes played on them.

The final client; remember James, the truck driver ? Sharon and James are my last two Sunshine Factory clients, they have brought their eight year old son with them. We reminisced over how scared he was to ask her to have a coffee with him. We agreed it was a fast passage of time. James now owned a fleet of long haul trucks. Finishing with Sharon and him, he asked if i would cut his son's hair. He told him never to forget this cut, that if it had not been for Don, he would not be here. James and i hugged, and said goodbye. Sometimes i did good !

SUMMATION

THE EIGHTIES

The 1980's was a time of stabilization a pause between two cataclysmic convulsions. The sexual emancipation began in mid century, and the Hi Tech explosion. My profession changed dramatically. The 'Star' image enjoyed in the 70's gave way to a new vibrant model, we were now business men and women. NOTE : A long, long way from when the wife of a politician runs for the presidency, she was a fund raiser for a charity representing the mentally handicapped. A reporter asked why she was so passionate about her cause. Her reply; a member of her family was mentally impaired, she could not attend college, but she could become a beautician.

College graduates, dissatisfied with their career choices enrolled in cosmetology schools. NOTE : In the final summation, you will be introduced to the innovations Paul Mitchell Systems offer in primary cosmetology education.

FASHION HAIR

Men in all professions felt free to choose the style that best represented them. There would never again, be a social standard. Women had reached fashion parity with men, they could wear Nike's to work. Anywhere from Main Street to Wall street.

THE SHANGRILA PASSAGES

168
/ 34

The 90's begin for me in June 1988. the 'Curve' being showcased in Paul Mitchell events around the world. I chose to re locate to Costa Rica with 20 Paul Mitchell events a year, down time was much needed between events, it was necessary to maintain a high level of skill.
The first health Spa in Costa Rica had just opened, a Canadian, and an American, both with degrees in exercise physiology, built a 'state of the art' facility. Convincing them a salon would enhance the Spa's image, space was made available, the best of both worlds, i could exercise, take a shower, lunch in the Spa's restaurant, and be hard at work by 1:00 P. M. all without leaving the premises.

169
/ 35

TICAS

In Costa Rica, men are referred to as 'Ticos', the women, 'Ticas' First day, First client. Carmen and me had previously become acquainted while working out.
Client : Carmen : Tuesday 1 : 00 P.M.
She is a Latin beauty, black hair in abundance, seldom found in the U.S. Black eyes, smoldering with passion. She is shampooed, we are discussing a new style. Her hair is one length, below her shoulders. "
Don, I see in fashion magazines that layered hair is the new look, what does layering mean ? " NOTE : in Costa Rica, hair was predominantly one length as in all of Latin America.
Explaining the advantages of layering, she says " Go for it. " ten minutes into the cut she says " May i ask you some questions ? "

" Sure. "   " Tell me about Californian girls, are they all tall, blonde, and sleep with different men but live on their own ? "   " Wait, wait, give me a minute to think. " the questions being asked with such candor was amusing. " They are tall, blonde, usually enhanced by their stylist, American women decide what their sexual needs are. They tend to leave home at an early age, often share apartments, sometimes with boyfriends, does that answer your questions ? " Carmen says " Yes, but Don, in the movies they seem to have so much trouble with their boyfriends, is that so. " " Yes, but they explore their personal needs and are un afraid to tell men what they want. " Carmen sighs, " I wish we could be a little like that, we are not very independent, we live with our parents until we marry, then, if we can afford it, we build a house, usually close to other family members, she pauses, sex before marriage is never talked about. Especially with parents ! " Don, are you familiar with 'Honeymoon Hotels' ? " " No, what are they ? "   " Young people use them when they are dating, here is how it works, you pull your car into a garage, close the garage door, then enter the motel room, there's a small hatch in the wall, you pay through this, no one ever sees you, and you don't sign a guest book. NOTE : During the next ten years, i learn much about the mating habits of the natives from her.

The finished product :

Carmen is standing in front of the mirror and vigorously shaking her head, a black 'Mane' cascades around her, " I love it ! " she exclaims. " All my friends will be in to see you. " she hugs me and kisses both my cheeks, not a 'Hollywood" air kiss, but the real thing. Oh ! did i mention, she was only wearing a bikini at the time !

Carmen was typical of her social structure, the Ticos, at that point in time treated their women just a little better than the Taliban ! they did not publicly stone them, it was far more subtle, they treated them like children regardless of their level of education. It was not to last. Beginning in the 90's the change far outpaced the women's movement in the U. S. in one decade, they advanced to a point their American 'Sisters' had taken forty years to achieve ! how was this accomplished ? they did not burn their bra's, they did not march in the streets. They used an approach no man since 'Adam' or 'Samson' could resist, they simply disarmed their men by loving them.

171
/ 39

171
/ 40

171
/ 41

172
/ 41

173
/ 42

Client : Rita, Friday 3: 00 P. M.
NOTE : First time clients are apprehensive, rules to put them at ease,
Never ask : ' How was your Day ? " they might have had a fight with
their 'Significant other' . Their broker called to tell them their 401/ K
tanked. The bathroom scales showed a 5Lb gain, there are any number
of things that could contribute to a client's 'Bad Day' They come to us to
restore their self esteem, and through our art of illusion, make them the
irresistible people they know they are.
Rita is a 5' 11" aerobic instructor. The Spa has reached the social
status of (Huxley's Brave New World) men and women in aerobic
classes are wearing work - out attire. Britney Spears and Christine
Aguilera in their M.T.V. videos, would in comparison, be overdressed !
Rita, having just finished an aerobic class, showered, and slipped into
a white stretch cotton 6 Oz. Dolce Gabon creation, ubiquitous three
inch heels, which all Latin women wear from the age of 10 ! she is a
vision. Rita is in my chair, " Don, I'm really tired of my long hair,
let's do something wild. " " How wild do you want ? " " Cut it all
really short, i have been having dreams about how my life will change
with a new image." NOTE : Clients have told me before that they
dreamed about a radical change and gone ahead with it because of that.
" I don't want to be a slave to my hair, Latin men love long hair, if
they don't love me with short hair, then fuck them ! " " O.K. here's
my suggestion, lets go to the max, cut it very short on the sides,
leave the top long, four inches, texturize it . this will give you
options, using Paul Mitchell gel, you can go spikey, or sleek. " Rita is
surprisingly calm as five years growth falls to the floor ! thirty
minutes later she is transformed. I chose to spike here hair.
She stands and stares at her new persona in the salon's full length
mirror, she is speechless. This is the only time in nearly two decades
of knowing her that Rita is lost for words ! she is un able to tear
herself away from the mirror. NOTE : During this personal re
evaluation, the client needs a quiet few moments to themselves. Male
clients can suffer trauma by simply changing the parting from one side to
the other ! When president Jimmy Carter changed his, it was headline
news for a week ! no one ever asked the right person as to why he had
done it, he himself gave a non committal answer. Any of us in the
profession could have answered why in an instant. He was suffering from
un even receding hairline and switched his parting to cover the increasing
baldness.
Rita begins to smile, and dance with the sensuality that only Latin
women can achieve. Her first words, the universal women's war cry,

" I'm going shopping " she hugs me and gives me a meaningful kiss. She strides out of the salon with an air that demands homage from lesser mortals. As she goes through the Spa restaurant, all conversation and movement has stopped ! it was a moment when time became elastic. A full two minutes before normality was restored. For me, this was an introduction to Costa Rican society. The next month was hyperactive ! the salon staff sheared fifty heads a day.

COMMENT

Tica's : cutting their was symbolic of a shift in women's self empowerment, divorce was no longer a taboo !
A popular president had a second family. He won the Nobel Peace Prize years later he was re-elected, all the while, the supposedly Liberal U.S. was trying to impeach a president for having felatio in the oval office.
  Client : Alle

Alle is a precocious sixteen year old with the body of a world class gymnast, unfortunately, Costa Rica does not have a gymnastic program.
While having lunch, Alle approaches me, and asks if she can join me, " It would be my pleasure. " I respond she takes a seat, and looks pensive for a moment. " Is there something you wish to ask ? "
  " Don, I want to become a professional trainer, do you think the hair should go ? " " Yes, most trainers in aerobic magazines have short hair, it is convenient and professional. " she thinks for a moment. " Now, Today, lets go for it ! " " I can fit you in at 3:00 P.M. be there."
Alle: 3:00 P.M.

She is shampooed and ready to go.
" What do you think will look 'hot' ? " she asks. "
Since lunch, i have been thinking, you should go extreme 'Grace Jones' the black rock star's psyche is close to yours. " " You mean a flat top ? " " You will be the first girl in Costa Rica to have one. "
" Do it " twenty minutes later, the contrast between the feminine sexual energy she projects and the 'Macho' Marine flat top is devastating ! I was amazed at the metamorphosis of this young butterfly, she was now a magnificent Eagle !
Over the next fifteen years, she soared from triumph to triumph

174
/ 43

174
/ 44

174
/ 45

COMMENT

Alle produced and starred in exercise videos, owned a successful Spa, opened a famous Paris franchise, dress salon, in her spare time ! she bred show horses . . . . no that's not all there's more ! she met her future husband in the salon. With regard to all her other adventures, my lips are sealed ! !

174 / 46

Client : Carmela : Wednesday : 1 : 30 P.M.

Carmela is an interviewer for a T.V. fashion weekly. She has decided to be adventurous. Her first color experience will be highlights. She has an ambition to re locate to Venezuela and become a 'Novella' T.V. actress (i.e. soap operas) at 5' 9" voluptuous with green eyes I can't see a problem !

Carmela's hair extends five inches below her shoulder. This will be an extended time process, made enjoyable by her infectious personality. " Don, I read in Cosmopolitan, stories about parties, do people really trade partners and they go nude in Jacuzzis ? " " Some people, yes, but not all. " " What about wife swapping clubs, is this true ? " " Yes, there are 'swinger' publications, you list what your preferences are and you will meet people with similar preferences. " " You know Don, it's crazy in Cost Rica, sexual freedom is non existent for women, yet prostitution is legal ! I believe my generation will change the social structure of Costa Rica. " she was right, Ticas became pro active, they demanded laws be passed that made divorce easier. Now, women are protected from sexual harassment in the work place.

176 / 49

Costa Rica has a female vice-president and cabinet members. What is remarkable, is that Ticas accomplished historical social changes in one generation,. Carmela moved to Argentina, became a 'Novela' Diva, got married and had children.

SUMMATION
COSTA RICA

In the late 90's, clients of both sexes they had different sexual values than their parents generation. Couples did swap, but they did not mix demographics. Singles stayed exclusive in their own groups. I have not delved into the morays of prostitution in Costa Rica, that is better left to sociologists, with no views on the subject, other than women and men should, without social stigma, be free to do as they wish with their bodies. Hopefully, they choose healthy practices.

OBITUARY

HEARALD TRIBUNE
By Margalit Fox 01 / 11 / 2008

Gerard Damiano, a hairdresser turned film maker, whose best known work " Deep Throat" created sensation in every possible meaning of the term when it was released in 1972, died on Saturday in Fort Myers Florida. He was 80 and had lived in Fort Myers in recent years. "The cause was complications of a stroke he had last month." his son Gerard Jnr. said.

Written and directed by Damiano under the name of Jerry Gerard, "Deep Throat" was pornography's 'Gone with the wind' in terms of grosses. The New York Times wrote in 1973 it attained emblematic status as one of the first hard-core films to reach a wide general audience, from self- conscious middle Americans to self congratulatory celebrities. "Porno Chic" the news media often called it.

Over three and a half decades, "Deep Throat" has been damned by religious groups, decried by feminists, defended by First Amendment advocates, derided by critics and debated by social scientists. It dragged for years through local and federal courts around the country in a welter of obscenity trials in which it was variously banned, un banned and re banned. All of this had the effect, observers agreed, of sustaining acute public interest in the film.

In what was perhaps the movie's most enduring legacy, it's title became the pseudonym of The Washington Post's clandestine source in it's coverage of the Watergate scandal. In 2005, W. Mark Felt, a former second in command at the Federal Bureau of Investigation identified himself as Deep Throat.

"Deep Throat" was shot in six days for not much more than 25,000 Dollars money put up, as has been widely reported by associates of the Colombo crime family. By 2005, it had grossed more than 600 Million Dollars. Entertainment Weekly reported. The films premise was medical in nature. It's attractive young heroine suffered from a condition previously un recorded in the annals of science, which The Times Magazine, in 1973 described as " an eccentricity of her anatomy" that caused her to find oral sex more gratifying than conventional intercourse."

With the film, Damiano, gave it's star, nee Linda Boreman, what is generally believed to be her first speaking role. He also bestowed upon her the screen name Linda Lovelace. In later years, Boreman denounced the film as depicting her "rape" she died in 2002 of injuries suffered in an auto accident.

CONCLUSION

The rate of change, beginning in the mid twentieth century has no equal in human history. By the century's end, women had parity with men, education, the work place and politics. Of all these, hard won equalities, their sexual self empowerment is, arguably, their greatest achievement. The fashion world was instrumental in breaking all the old taboos. Coco Chanel, took women from whalebone corsets to the ubiquitious 'little black dress' Mary Quant gave us the 'Mini skirt' Kinsey / Masters and Johnson gave us the freedom to discuss sex both publicly and privately. Conversations in the salon encompassed all of the above.

My world of esoteric fashion contributed equally Kenneth (Jackie Kennedy's hairdresser) introduced the Bouffant, Vidal Sassoon, The Shag, Paul Mitchell Systems , Hair care products, liquid styling tools, and education. In parting, be kind to your hairdresser !

NOTE : To all sentient beings who purchase this tome , I want you to know that a portion of sales will be awarded, as scholarships, to Paul Mitchell (the school)

NOTE : J.P. if you find merit in this work (of three LONG years) information regarding applying for the scholarship can be added at this point.

"My days working with Paul Mitchell , Jeanne Braa , John Paul and the new kid Robert Cromens as well as Floyd Kenyatta where a delight to say the least. So many new things where happening my head was spinning. One of the coolest times of this period was meeting and working with Don Davis who has since become a life long friend , Being asked to introduce his Curved comb set was not only a different approach to cutting hair but also using a clipper to do so which at that time few hairdressers where doing so. I first met Don at his Sunshine factory in San Diego where as a member of the JPMS Show team we where along with 3 or 4 others being trained how to use the Curves and the thought Process behind it. As soon as i was introduced to Don i knew we would be friends for life , He just has that way about him. To this day we are in constant contact. I am very excited to see the Naked Hairdresser Finely be made into book form. This is a tell all Book about our Fab industry from the revolution in the 60's on. I am delighted to be part of this and to be included as well , Thank you Don and much Love to you my friend, Carry on sweet man and as always my best to you"

"Albie Mulcahy"

41751774R00073

Made in the USA
San Bernardino, CA
05 July 2019